Fodor's 93 Pocket New York City

Reprinted from *Fodor's New York City '93*

Fodor's Travel Publications, Inc.
New York • Toronto • London •
Sydney • Auckland

ISBN 0-679-02328-3

Fodor's Pocket New York City

Editor: Holly Hughes
Contributors: Jane Hershey, Marcy Pritchard, Terry Trucco
Creative Director: Fabrizio La Rocca
Cartographer: David Lindroth
Illustrator: Karl Tanner
Cover Photograph: Owen Franken
Design: Vignelli Associates

Special Sales

Fodor's Travel Publications are available at special discounts for bulk purchases (100 copies or more) for sales promotions or premiums. Special editions, including personalized covers, excerpts of existing guides, and corporate imprints, can be created in large quantities for special needs. For more information write to Special Marketing, Fodor's Travel Publications, 201 East 50th St., New York, NY 10022; Random House of Canada, Ltd., Marketing Department, 1265 Aerowood Drive, Mississauga, Ontario L4W 1B9; or Fodor's Travel Publications, 20 Vauxhall Bridge Rd., London, England SW1V 2SA.

Contents

Maps

Foreword

While every care has been taken to ensure the accuracy of the information in this guide, the passage of time will always bring change, and consequently, the publisher cannot accept responsibility for errors that may occur.

All prices and opening times quoted here are based on information supplied to us at press time. Hours and admission fees may change, however, and the prudent traveler will avoid inconvenience by calling ahead.

Fodor's wants to hear about your travel experiences, both pleasant and unpleasant. When a hotel or restaurant fails to live up to its billing, let us know and we will investigate the complaint and revise our entries where the facts warrant it.

Send your letters to the editors of Fodor's Travel Publications, 201 E. 50th Street, New York, NY 10022.

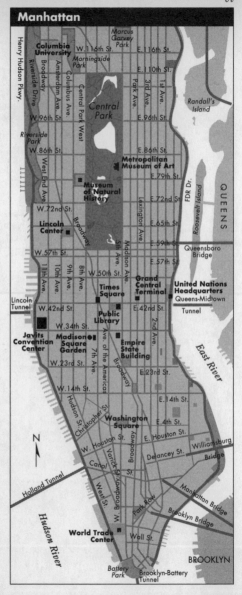

Manhattan

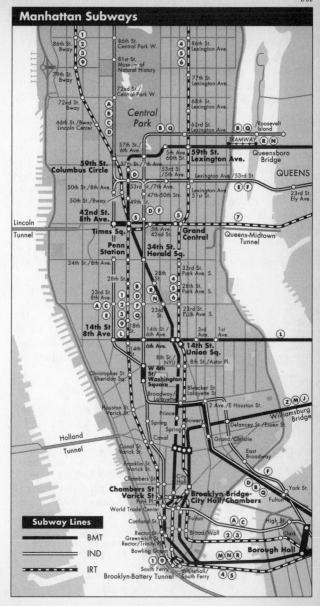

Manhattan Subways

Introduction

By Michael Adams

Senior writer for the business travel magazine Successful Meetings, *Michael Adams finally moved to his hometown, New York City, 12 years ago.*

In 1925, the youthful songwriting team of Richard Rodgers and Larry Hart wrote "Manhattan," arguably the loveliest city anthem ever. "We'll have Manhattan, the Bronx, and Staten Island, too," it promises, drawing its images from the merry scramble that was the city more than 60 years ago: "sweet pushcarts," "baloney on a roll," a subway that "charms," Brighton Beach, Coney Island, and the popular comedy *Abie's Irish Rose*. "We'll turn Manhattan into an isle of joy," coos the refrain.

Several decades later, in 1989, an album called simply *New York*, by aging enfant terrible rocker Lou Reed, views the same city with glasses fogged by despair and cynicism: Drugs, crime, racism, and promiscuity reign in what Reed considers to be a sinkhole of "crudity, cruelty of thought and sound." His voice brittle with weary irony, he sings, "This is no time for celebration." Manhattan's "sweet pushcarts" now apparently overflow with deadly vials of crack.

So, whom to believe—Lou or Larry?

The truth of the matter is slippery, for New York has long been a mosaic of grand contradictions, a city for which there has never been—nor ever will be—a clear consensus. Hart himself took the city to task in another song, "Give It Back to the Indians," whose lyrics count off a litany of problems that still exist: crime, dirt, high prices, traffic jams, and all-around urban chaos. Yet for all that, millions live here, grumbling but happy, and millions more visit, curious as cats to find out what the magnificent fuss is all about.

I was in eighth grade in suburban Detroit when I first really became aware of New

York. A friend's Manhattan-born mother still subscribed to the Sunday *New York Times*, and at their house I'd pore over the "Arts and Leisure" section, as rapt as an archaeologist with a cave painting. The details of what I read there have blurred, but I remember vividly the sensation I felt while reading: a combined anticipation and nostalgia so keen it bordered on pain. Although I had never been there, I was homesick for New York.

It's my home now, yet I can still understand and appreciate the impulse that draws visitors here. In a city so ripe with possibilities, we are all more or less visitors.

I think of this on an uncharacteristically warm day in late March, as I and fellow New Yorkers escape from the hives of offices and homes to celebrate spring's first preview. We unbutton our jackets, leave buses a stop or two before our usual destinations, quicken our resolve to visit that new exhibit at the Met or jog around the Central Park Reservoir. A jubilant sense of renewal infects us all, and I overhear one happy fellow saying to a friend, "I felt just like a tourist yesterday."

Whenever I get the New York blues, the best tonic for me is to glimpse the city through the eyes of a visitor. One day, after subway construction had rerouted me well out of my usual path, I found myself in the grimy Times Square station—hardly the place for a spiritual conversion. As usual I had that armor of body language that we New Yorkers reflexively assume to protect ourselves from strangers bent on (1) ripping us off, (2) doing us bodily harm, (3) converting us, (4) making sexual advances, or (5) being general pains-in-the-butt just for the hell of it. But that day, tucked away in a corner, was a group of musicians—not an uncommon sight in New York—playing the guitar, organ, and accordion with gusto and good spirits behind a homemade sign that dubbed them the "Argentinian Tango Company." Like many street musicians in Manhattan, they were *good*, but I was only half listening, too intent on cursing the city. Just as I passed the band, however, I noticed four teenagers drawn to the music—visitors surely, they were far too open and trusting to be anything else. Grinning as widely as the Argentinians, they began to perform a spontaneous imitation of flamenco dancing—clapping hands above their heads, raising their heels, laughing at themselves, and only slightly self-conscious. Passersby, myself included, broke into smiles. As I made my way to the subway platform, buoyed by the impromptu show, I once again forgave New York. This minor piece of magic was apology enough.

I wonder whether that was the moment one of those teenagers happened to fall in love with the city. It *can* happen in a single moment, to a visitor or to a longtime resident. Perhaps it hits during a stroll through Riverside Park after a blanketing snowfall, when trees have turned to crystal and the city feels a hush it knows at no other time; or when you turn a corner and spy, beyond a phalanx of RVs and a tangle of cables and high-beam lights, the filming of a new movie.

That moment could also come when the house lights begin to dim at the Metropolitan Opera, and the gaudily sparkling chandeliers make their magisterial ascent to the ceiling; or when you first glimpse the magnificently bright Prometheus statue in Rockefeller Center, gleaming like a giant present under the annual Christmas tree as dozens of skaters cut swirls of seasonal colors on the ice below. You may even be smitten in that instant when, walking along the streets in the haze of a summer afternoon, you look up above the sea of anonymous faces to see—and be astonished by—the lofty rows of skyscrapers, splendid in their arrogance and power. At times like these it is perfectly permissible to stop for a moment, take a breath, and think, "Wow! *This is New York!*" We who live here do it every so often ourselves.

For some, of course, that special moment comes with a happy shock of recognition when they spot a street or building made familiar by movies or television, anything from *I Love Lucy* to *On the Waterfront.* At the Empire State Building, who can help but remember King Kong's pathetically courageous swing from its pinnacle? Or at the brooding Dakota, the chilling destiny created for Rosemary's baby within those fortresslike walls? In the mind's eye, Audrey Hepburn is eternally pairing diamonds and a doughnut as she wends her swank way down Fifth Avenue to have breakfast at Tiffany's. And the miniature park on Sutton Place will always be where Woody Allen and Diane Keaton began their angst-ridden *Manhattan* love affair, with the 59th Street bridge gleaming beyond and Gershwin music swelling in the background.

There's a moment of sudden magic when a New York stereotype, seen so often on screen that it seems a joke, suddenly comes to life: when a gum-cracking waitress calls you "hon," or a stogie-sucking cabbie asks, "How 'bout them Yankees, Mac?" There's also the thrill of discovering one of New York's cities-within-the-city: Mulberry Street in Little Italy; Mott Street in Chinatown; Park Avenue's enclave of wealth and privilege; SoHo and TriBeCa, with their artistic types dressed in black from head to toe; or Sheridan Square, the nexus of the city's prominent lesbian and gay communities. The first glimpse of a landmark could begin the visitor's infatuation, too: frenetic Grand Central Station, abustle with suburban commuters; the concrete caverns of Wall Street, throbbing with power and ambition; or the Statue of Liberty, which neither cliché nor cheap souvenir can render common.

As you ready yourself to take on New York's contradictions, prepare to wonder and to exult. Here, on a single day, you might catch a glimpse of Jacqueline Onassis—she's been known to stop at Burger Heaven and have lunch at the counter—or Rollerena, the gloriously tacky drag-queen-cum-fairy-godmother on roller skates, who waves her magic wand to bestow blessings on select public events. Here you can eat sumptuously at a hot dog stand or at a world-celebrated gourmet shrine.

Excess and deprivation mingle here: As a limousine crawls lazily to take its pampered passengers to their luxe destination, it rolls past a threadbare beggar seeking the warmth that steams from the city's belly through an iron grate. It's a ludicrously bright cartoon and a sobering documentary, New York—almost too much for one city to be. It's maddening and it's thrilling; monstrous, yet beautiful beyond parallel.

And I envy anyone their first taste of it.

1 Essential Information

Before You Go

Visitor Information

The **New York Convention and Visitors Bureau** (2 Columbus Circle, New York, NY 10019, tel. 212/397–8222) provides a wealth of free information, including brochures, subway and bus maps, an up-to-date calendar of events, listings of hotels and weekend hotel packages, and discount coupons for Broadway shows. **The New York Division of Tourism** (1 Commerce Plaza, Albany, NY 12245, tel. 518/474–4116 or 800/225–5697) offers a free series of "I Love New York" booklets listing attractions and tour packages available in New York City.

Tips for British Travelers

Government Tourist Office

Contact the **State of New York Division of Tourism** (2 Cinnamon Row, Plantation Wharf, York Place, London SW11 3TW, tel. 071/978–5275) for brochures and tourist information.

Passports and Visas

You will need a valid, 10-year passport (cost £15) to enter the United States. You do not need a visa if you are staying for less than 90 days and have a return ticket on a major airline. There are some exceptions to this, so check with your travel agent or with the **United States Embassy** (Visa and Immigration Department, 5 Upper Grosvenor St., London W1A 2JB, tel. 071/499–3443). No vaccinations are needed for entry into the United States.

Customs

Entering the United States, you may bring 200 cigarettes, 50 cigars, or 2 kilograms tobacco; 1 liter of alcohol; duty-free gifts up to a value of $100. Be careful not to take in meat or meat products, seeds, plants, fruits, etc. Absolutely avoid illegal drugs.

Returning to the United Kingdom, you may take home, if you are 17 or older: (1) 200 cigarettes, 100 cigarillos, 50 cigars, or 250 grams of tobacco; (2) 2 liters of table wine and (a) 1 liter of alcohol over 22% by volume (most spirits), (b) 2 liters of alcohol under 22% by volume (fortified or sparkling wine), or (c) 2 more liters of table wine; (3) 60 milliliters of perfume and 250 milliliters of toilet water; and (4) other goods up to a value of £32, but no more than 50 liters of beer or 25 lighters.

Insurance We recommend that to cover health and motoring mishaps, you insure yourself with **Europ Assistance** (252 High St., Croydon, Surrey CR0 1NF, tel. 081/680–1234). It is also wise to take out insurance to cover lost luggage (if your current homeowners' policies don't cover such loss). Trip-cancellation insurance is also a good idea. **The Association of British Insurers** (Aldermary House, 10–15 Queen St., London EC4N 1TT, tel. 071/248–4477) will give you comprehensive advice on all aspects of holiday insurance.

Tour Operators The on-again, off-again price battle over transatlantic fares has meant that most tour operators now offer excellent budget packages to the United States. Among those you might consider as you plan your trip are:

Albany Travel (Manchester) Ltd. (Central Buildings, 211 Deansgate, Manchester M2 5QR, tel. 061/833–0202).

American Airplan (Airplan House, Churchfield Rd., Walton-on-Thames, Surrey KT12 2TJ, tel. 0932/231422 for information, 0932/246347 for brochures).

American Travel Centre (77 Victoria St., Windsor, Berkshire SL4 1EH, tel. 0753/831300).

Cosmosair plc (Ground Floor, Dale House, Tiviot Dale, Stockport, Cheshire SK1 1TB, tel. 061/480–5799).

Jetsave (Sussex House, London Rd., East Grinstead, Sussex RH19 1LD, tel. 0342/312033).

Speedbird Holidays (Pacific House, Hazelwick Ave., Crawley, W. Sussex RH10 1NP, tel. 0293/611611).

Thomas Cook Ltd. (Box 36, Thorpe Wood, Peterborough PE3 6SB, tel. 0733/332333).

Airfares Airlines flying to New York include **British Airways, TWA, Continental,** and **Virgin Atlantic.** At press time, a low-season return APEX fare was anywhere from £419 and up. If you are flexible with your travel dates, Virgin Atlantic offers a Late Saver fare from £349, but it can only be booked three days before departure.

Thomas Cook Ltd. can often book you on cut-price flights. Call the Cook branch nearest you and ask about their Flightsavers program. Be sure to call at least 21 days in advance of when you want to travel.

Also check out the small ads in magazines such as *Time Out* and in the Sunday papers, where flights are offered for as low as £199 return.

What to Pack

New York City has a number of restaurants that require men to wear jackets and ties. For sightseeing and casual dining, jeans and sneakers are acceptable just about anywhere in the city. Sneakers or other flat-heeled walking shoes are highly recommended for pounding the New York pavements; you may even see business-people in button-down office attire lacing them on for the sprint from one appointment to another.

An extra pair of glasses, contact lenses, or prescription sunglasses is always a good idea; it is important to pack any prescription medicines you use regularly, as well as any allergy medication you may need.

Pack light, because porters and luggage trolleys can be hard to find at New York airports. You may need a fistful of quarters to rent a trolley, if no personnel are on duty by the coin-operated trolley racks.

Carry-on Luggage Passengers on U.S. airlines are limited to two carry-on bags. For a bag you wish to store under the seat, the maximum dimensions are 9″ × 14″ × 22″. For bags that can be hung in a closet or on a luggage rack, the maximum dimensions are 4″ × 23″ × 45″. For bags you wish to store in an overhead bin, the maximum dimensions are 10″ × 14″ × 36″. An airline can adapt the rules to circumstances, so on a crowded flight you may be allowed only one carry-on bag. In addition to carryons, you may bring aboard a handbag (pocketbook or purse); an overcoat or wrap; an umbrella; a camera; a reasonable amount of reading material; an infant bag; and crutches, a cane, braces, or other prosthetic device. Infant/child safety seats can also be brought aboard if parents have purchased a ticket for the child, or if there is space in the cabin.

Foreign airlines generally allow only one piece of carry-on luggage in tourist class, in addition to handbags and bags filled with duty-free goods. Passengers in first and business class are allowed to carry on one garment bag as well. Call your airline to find out its current policy.

Checked Luggage Luggage allowances vary slightly from airline to airline. Many carriers allow three checked pieces, but some allow only two, so check before you go. In all cases, check-in luggage cannot weigh more than 70 pounds per piece or be larger than 62 inches (length + width + height).

Arriving and Departing

By Plane

Airports Virtually every major U.S. and foreign airline serves one or more of New York's three airports: **La Guardia Airport** and **John F. Kennedy International Airport,** both in the borough of Queens, and **Newark International Airport** in New Jersey.

Airlines U.S. carriers serving the New York area include America West (tel. 800/247–5692); American (tel. 800/433–7300); Continental (tel. 800/525–0280); Delta (tel. 800/221–1212); Northwest (tel. 800/225–2525); TWA (tel. 800/221–2000); United (tel. 800/241–6522); and USAir (tel. 800/428–4322).

When choosing a flight, be sure to distinguish among (a) *nonstop flights*—no stops or changes of aircraft; (b) *direct flights*—one or more stops but no change of aircraft; and (c) *connecting flights*—at least one change of aircraft and possibly several stops as well.

Between the Airports and Manhattan *La Guardia Airport* Taxis cost $18–$23 plus tolls (which may be as high as $4) and take 20–40 minutes. Group taxi rides to Manhattan are available at taxi dispatch lines just outside the baggage-claim areas during most travel hours (except on Saturdays and holidays). Group fares run $8–$9 per person (plus a share of tolls) depending on your destination.

Carey Airport Express buses (tel. 800/456–1012, 800/284–0909, or 718/632–0500) depart for Manhattan every 20 minutes from 6 AM to midnight. It's a 20- to 30-minute ride to 42nd Street and Park Avenue, directly opposite Grand Central Terminal. The bus continues from there to the Port Authority Bus Terminal, the New York Hilton, Sheraton Manhattan, Crowne Plaza Holiday Inn, and Marriott Marquis hotels. Other midtown hotels are a short cab ride away. The bus fare is $8.50 ($10 to the hotels); pay the driver. **The Gray Line Air Shuttle Minibus** (tel. 212/757–6840) serves major Manhattan hotels directly to and from the airport. The fare is $12 per person; make arrangements at the airport's ground transportation center or use the courtesy phone.

JFK International Airport **Taxis** cost $25–$30 plus tolls (which may be as much as $4) and take 35–60 minutes.

Carey Airport Express buses (tel. 800/456–1012, 800/284–0909, or 718/632–0500) depart for Manhattan every 30 minutes from 6 AM to midnight, from all JFK terminals. The ride to 42nd Street and Park Avenue (Grand Central Terminal) takes about one hour. The bus continues from there to the Port Authority Bus Terminal, the New York Hilton, Sheraton Manhattan, Crowne Plaza Holiday Inn, and Marriott Marquis hotels; it's a short cab ride to other midtown hotels. The bus fare is $11 ($12.50 to the hotels); pay the driver.

The Gray Line Air Shuttle Minibus (tel. 212/757–6840) serves major Manhattan hotels directly from the airport; the cost is $15 per person. Make arrangements at the airport's ground transportation counter or use the courtesy phone.

Newark Airport **Taxis** cost $28–$30 plus tolls ($4) and take 20–45 minutes. "Share and Save" group rates are available for up to four passengers between 8 AM and midnight; make arrangements with the airport's taxi dispatcher.

NJ Transit Airport Express buses (tel. 201/762–5100) depart every 15–30 minutes for the Port Authority Bus Terminal, at Eighth Avenue and 42nd Street. From there it's a short cab ride to midtown hotels. The ride takes 30–45 minutes. The fare is $7; buy your ticket inside the airport terminal.

Olympia Airport Express buses (tel. 212/964–6233) leave for Grand Central Terminal, Penn Station, and 1 World Trade Center (next to the Vista hotel) about every 30 minutes from around 6 AM to midnight. The trip takes 35–45 minutes to Grand Central and Penn Station, 20 minutes to WTC. The fare is $7.

The Gray Line Air Shuttle Minibus (tel. 212/757–6840) serves major Manhattan hotels directly to and from the airport. You pay $17 per passenger; make arrangements at the airport's ground transportation center or use the courtesy phone.

By Car

The **Lincoln Tunnel** (I–495), **Holland Tunnel,** and **George Washington Bridge** (I–95) connect Manhattan with the New Jersey Turnpike system and points west. The Lincoln Tunnel comes into midtown Manhattan; the Holland Tunnel into lower Manhattan; and the George Washington Bridge into northern Manhattan. Each of the three arteries requires a toll ($4 for cars) eastbound into New York, but no toll westbound.

From upstate New York, the city is accessible via the **New York (Dewey) Thruway** (I–87) (toll) to the **Major Deegan Expressway** (I–87) through the Bronx and across the **Triborough Bridge** ($2.50 toll), or via the **Taconic State Parkway** to the **Saw Mill River Parkway** ($1.25 toll bridge) into upper Manhattan.

From New England, the **Connecticut Turnpike** (I–95) connects with the **New England Thruway** (I–95) and then the **Bruckner Expressway** (I–278). Take the Bruckner to the **Triborough Bridge** ($2.50 toll) or to the **Cross Bronx Expressway,** which enters upper Manhattan on the west side ($1.25 toll bridge).

Manhattan has two major north–south arteries that run the length of the island. The **West Side Highway** skirts the Hudson River from Battery Park (where it's known as West Street) through midtown (it then becomes the Henry Hudson Parkway north of 72nd Street) and past the George Washington Bridge. Both the Holland and Lincoln tunnels enter Manhattan just a few blocks east of this route; the Cross Bronx Expressway connects with the Henry Hudson Parkway in northern Manhattan at the George Washington Bridge. **Franklin D. Roosevelt Drive** (FDR Drive) runs along the East River from Battery Park into upper Manhattan, where it becomes Harlem River Drive north of 125th Street. Both the Queens Midtown Tunnel (East 36th Street) and the Queensboro Bridge (East 59th Street) can be entered a few blocks west of FDR Drive, which connects with the Triborough Bridge at East 125th Street.

Be forewarned: The deterioration of the bridges linking Manhattan, especially those spanning the East River, is a serious problem, and repairs will be ongoing for the next few years. Don't be surprised if a bridge is all or partially closed.

Driving within Manhattan can be a nightmare of gridlocked streets and predatory motorists. Free parking is difficult to find in midtown, and violators may be towed away literally within minutes. All over town, parking lots charge exorbitant rates—as much as $15 for two hours in some neighborhoods. If you do drive, don't plan to use your car much for traveling within Manhattan.

Car Rentals

If you find you absolutely need a car—perhaps for a weekend escape or because Manhattan is part of a longer trip—you'll have to sort out Manhattan's confusing array of car-rental possibilities. Although rates were once cheaper out of Newark airport, that is no longer the case; prices charged by national firms are the same at Newark, Kennedy, and La Guardia, as well as at Manhattan rental locations. For a subcompact, expect to pay $50–$80 per day, with unlimited mileage. Companies with multiple Manhattan and airport locations include **Avis** (tel. 800/331–1212); **Budget** (tel. 800/527–0700); **Dollar** (tel. 800/800–4000); **Hertz** (tel. 800/654–3131); **National** (tel. 800/328–4567); and **Thrifty** (tel. 800/

367–2277). Some regional budget companies, such as **Rent-A-Wreck** (tel. 212/721–0080), offer lower rates. If you are flying into LaGuardia or Kennedy, you might look into some local Queens agencies with lower rates, such as **Universal** (tel. 718/786–0786). **Sunshine Rent-A-Car** (tel. 212/989–7260) is good for budget rentals in Greenwich Village.

Whomever you rent from, get a reservation number and ask whether there is free mileage and whether you must pay for a full tank of gas even if you don't use it.

By Train

Amtrak (tel. 800/872–7245) offers frequent service within the Northeast Corridor, between Boston and Washington, DC. Trains arrive at and depart from **Pennsylvania Station** (31st–33rd Sts., between 7th and 8th Aves.). Amtrak trains serve Penn Station from upstate New York, Montreal, the Southeast, Midwest, and Far West. Penn Station also handles **Long Island Railroad** trains (tel. 718/217–5477), with service to and from all over Long Island, and **New Jersey Transit** trains (tel. 201/762–5100), with frequent service from the northern and central regions of New Jersey.

Metro-North Commuter Railroad (tel. 212/532–4900) serves the northern suburbs and Connecticut from Grand Central Terminal as far east as New Haven. The other Metro-North Manhattan stop is at 125th Street and Park Avenue in East Harlem—not a good place to get off the train unless you are visiting this neighborhood.

PATH Trains (tel. 800/234–7284) run 24 hours a day to New York City from terminals in Hoboken, Jersey City, Harrison, and Newark, New Jersey; they connect with seven major New Jersey Transit commuter lines at Hoboken Station, Broad Street Station (Newark), and Penn Station (Newark). PATH trains stop in Manhattan at the World Trade Center and along Sixth Avenue at Christopher Street, 9th Street, 14th Street, 23rd Street, and 33rd Street. They run every 10 minutes on weekdays, every 15–30 minutes on weeknights, and every 20–30 minutes on weekends. The fare is $1.

By Bus

All long-haul and commuter bus lines feed into the **Port Authority Terminal,** a mammoth multi-level structure that occupies a nearly 2-square-block area between 40th and 42nd streets and Eighth and Ninth avenues. Though it was recently modernized and is fairly clean, large numbers of vagrants make the terminal an uncomfortable place to spend much time. Especially with night arrivals, plan to move through the terminal swiftly. Beware of hustlers trying to help you hail a cab on Eighth Avenue—they will demand a tip for performing this unnecessary service and can be hostile and aggressive if crossed.

For information on any service into or out of the Port Authority Terminal, call 212/564–8484. Some of the individual bus lines serving New York include **Greyhound-Trailways** (consult local information for a number in your area); **Adirondack Pine Hill Trailways** from upstate New York (tel. 800/225–6815); **Bonanza Bus Lines** from New England (tel. 800/556–3815); **Martz Trailways** from northeastern Pennsylvania (tel. 800/233–8604); **New Jersey Transit** from around New Jersey (tel. 201/762–5100); **Peter Pan Bus Lines** from New England (tel. 413/781–2900); and **Vermont Transit** from New England (tel. 802/862–9671).

Staying in New York

Important Addresses and Numbers

Tourist Information
New York Convention and Visitors Bureau. The main office is at 2 Columbus Circle (tel. 212/397–8222) and is open weekdays 9–6, weekends 10–6.

Emergencies
Dial 911 for **police, fire,** or **ambulance** in an emergency.

Deaf Emergency Teletypewriter (tel. 800/342–4357), for medical, fire, and ambulance emergencies.

Doctor **Doctors On Call**, 24-hour house-call service (tel. 212/737–2333). Near midtown, 24-hour emergency rooms are open at **St. Luke's-Roosevelt Hospital** (58th St. at 9th Ave., tel. 212/523–6800) and **St. Vincent's Hospital** (7th Ave. and 11th St., tel. 212/790–7997).

Dentist The **Dental Emergency Service** (tel. 212/679–3966; after 8 PM, tel. 212/679–4172) will make a referral.

24-Hour Pharmacy **Kaufman's Pharmacy** (Lexington Ave. and 50th St., tel. 212/755–2266).

Getting Around

By Subway The 230-mile subway system operates 24 hours a day and, especially within Manhattan, serves most of the places you'll want to visit. It's cheaper than a cab and, during the workweek, often faster than either cabs or buses. The trains have finally been rid of their graffiti (some New Yorkers, of course, perversely miss the colorful old trains) and sleek new air-conditioned cars predominate on many lines. The New York subway deserves much of its negative image, however. Many trains are crowded, dirty, and noisy, and even occasionally unsafe. Although trains are scheduled to run frequently, especially during rush hours, you never know when some incident somewhere on the line may stall traffic indefinitely. Unsavory characters lurk around certain stations, and panhandlers frequently work their way through the cars. Don't write off the subway—some 3.5 million passengers ride it every day without incident—but stay alert at all times.

The subway fare at press time was $1.25, but transit authority officials were already predicting that it should be raised to $1.40 or even $1.50, which may have occurred by the time you visit New York. Reduced fares are available for handicapped people and senior citizens during nonrush hours; children under 6 ride free. You must use a token to enter; they are sold at token booths that are *usually* open at each station. It's advisable to buy several tokens at one time to prevent waiting in line later (it always seems the lines are longest just as your train is roaring into the station). A token permits unlimited transfers within the system.

This book's subway map covers the most-visited parts of Manhattan. Maps of the full subway system are posted on many trains and at some stations, but don't rely on finding one when you need it. You may be able to pick up free maps at token booths, too, but they are often out of stock. Make sure the map you refer to is up-to-date—lengthy repair programs can cause reroutings that last long enough for new "temporary" maps to be printed.

Most midtown stops are crowded until fairly late at night, so for safety's sake, stay among the crowds on the center of the platforms. Avoid empty or nearly empty cars. During off-peak hours, try to ride in the same car as the conductor: It will stop near a line of light bulbs mounted above the edge of the platform. When disembarking from a train, stick with the crowd until you reach the comparative safety of the street.

By Bus Most buses follow easy-to-understand routes along the Manhattan grid. Routes go up or down the north–south avenues, or east and west on the major two-way crosstown streets. Most bus routes operate 24 hours, but service is infrequent late at night. Buses are great for sightseeing, but traffic jams—a potential threat at any time or place in Manhattan—can make rides maddeningly slow.

Bus fare is the same as subway fare: $1.25 at press time, in coins (no pennies; no change is given) or a subway token. When you get on the bus you can ask the driver for a free transfer coupon, good for one change to an intersecting route. Legal transfer points are listed on the back of the slip. Transfers have time limits of at least two hours, often longer. You cannot use the transfer to enter the subway system.

Guide-A-Rides, which consist of route maps and schedules, are posted at many bus stops in Manhattan and at major stops throughout the other boroughs. Each of the five boroughs of New York has a separate bus map, and they are scarcer than hens' teeth. They are occasionally available in subway token booths, but never on buses. The best places to obtain them are the Convention and Visitors Bureau at Columbus Circle or the information kiosks in Grand Central Terminal and Penn Station.

By Taxi Taxis are usually easy to hail on the street or from a taxi rank in front of major hotels. You can tell if a cab is available by checking its rooftop light; if the center panel is lit, the driver is ready to take passengers. Taxis cost $1.50 for the first ⅕ of a mile, 25¢ for each ⅕ of a mile thereafter, and 25¢ for each 75 seconds not in motion. A 50¢ surcharge is added to rides begun between 8 PM and 6 AM. There is no charge for extra passengers, but you must pay any bridge or tunnel tolls incurred during your trip (sometimes a driver will personally pay a toll to keep moving quickly, but that amount will be added to the fare when the ride is over). Taxi drivers also expect a 15% tip. Barring performance above and beyond the call of duty, don't feel obliged to give them more.

To avoid unhappy taxi experiences, try to have a general idea of where you want to go. A few cab drivers are dishonest; some are ignorant; some can barely understand English. If you have no idea of the proper route, you may be taken for a long and costly ride.

By Trolley The **Manhattan Neighborhood Trolley** (Box 1053, Knickerbocker Station, New York, NY 10002, tel. 212/677–7268), a 1900 vintage red-and-green car seating 30 passengers, runs weekends and holidays, noon–6 PM, April through October, making stops every hour at South Street Seaport, Battery Park, the World Trade Center, the World Financial Center, City Hall Park, Chatham Square in Chinatown, Grand Street in Little Italy, and Orchard Street on the Lower East Side. Tickets, which are valid for boarding and reboarding all day, cost $4 for adults, $3 for senior citizens and children under age 12, and may be purchased from a tour guide on board, who provides a running narration.

Guided Tours

Orientation Tours

Boat Tours

The most pleasant way to get a crash orientation to Manhattan is aboard a **Circle Line Cruise.** Once you've finished the three-hour, 35-mile circumnavigation of Manhattan, you'll have a good idea of where things are and what you want to see next. Narrations are as interesting and individualized as the guides who deliver them. *Pier 83, west end of 42nd St., tel. 212/563–3200. Fare: $16 adults, $8 children under 12. Operates early Mar.–Dec., daily.*

For a shorter excursion, the **TNT Express,** a hydroliner, will show you the island of Manhattan in 75 minutes. *Pier 11, 2 blocks south of South Street Seaport, tel. 800/342–5868. Fare: $15 adults, $13 senior citizens, $8 children under 12, children under 5 free. Boats depart Apr.–Sept, weekdays and Sat. at noon and 2 PM.*

World Yacht Cruises (Pier 81, W. 42nd St. at Hudson River, tel. 212/630–8100) serve lunch ($27.50) and Sunday brunch ($39.95) on two-hour cruises, and dinner ($62–$69.50) on three-hour cruises. The Continental cuisine is restaurant quality, and there's even music and dancing on board. The cruises run daily year-round.

The Spirit of New York (Pier 9, three blocks south of South Street Seaport on East River, tel. 212/742–7278) sails on lunch ($22.95), brunch ($29.95), dinner ($42.95–$48.95), and moonlight cocktail ($18) cruises.

At South Street Seaport's Pier 16 you can take two- or three-hour voyages to New York's past aboard the iron cargo schooner *Pioneer* or 90-minute tours of New York Harbor aboard the sidewheeler *Andrew Fletcher* or the *DeWitt Clinton,* a re-created steamboat. *Tel. 212/669–9400.*

Bus Tours   **Gray Line** (254 W. 54th St., tel. 212/397–2620) offers a number of standard city bus tours, plus cruises and day trips to Brooklyn and Atlantic City. **Short Line Tours** (166 W. 46th St., tel. 212/354–4740) offers some 20 different tour options.

Helicopter Tours **Island Helicopter** (heliport at E. 34th St. and East River, tel. 212/683–4575) offers four fly-over options, from $41 (for 7 miles) to $94 (for 35 miles). From the West Side, **Liberty Helicopter Tours** (heliport at W. 30th St. and Hudson River, tel. 212/465–8905) has three tours ranging from $55 to $119.

Special-Interest Tours **Backstage on Broadway** (tel. 212/575–8065) is a talk about the Broadway theater held in an actual theater, given by a theater professional. Reservations are mandatory; groups of 25 or more only. **Stardom Tours** (tel. 800/STARDOM) offers a tour around the city emphasizing celebrity homes and memorable movie locations. **Art Tours of Manhattan** (tel. 609/921–2647) custom-designs tours of museum and gallery exhibits as well as artists' studios and lofts. **Gallery Passports** (tel. 212/288–3578) takes you to galleries and museums in Manhattan. **Doorway to Design** (tel. 212/221–1111) tours fashion and interior design showrooms as well as artists' private studios. **Harlem Your Way!** (tel. 212/690–1687), **Harlem Spirituals, Inc.** (tel. 212/757–0425), and **Penny Sightseeing Co., Inc.** (tel. 212/410–0080) offer bus and walking tours and Sunday gospel trips to Harlem. **The Lower East Side Tenement Museum** (tel. 212/431–0233) offers Sunday tours through former immigrant communities. **River to River Downtown Tours** (tel 212/321–2823) specializes in lower Manhattan for two-hour walking tours. **Fulton Fish Market** tours give an insider's view of the early morning seafood market (tour guide Richard Lord, tel. 201/798–3901).

Walking Tours **Sidewalks of New York** (tel. 212/517–0201) hits the streets from various thematic angles—Ye Old Tavern tours, Celebrity Home tours, Famous Murder Sites, Chelsea Saints and Sinners, and so forth. These walks are offered on weekends year-round; weekday tours are available by appointment. **Adventure on a Shoestring** (tel. 212/265–2663) is an organization dating from 1963 that explores New York neighborhoods. Tours are scheduled periodically for $5 per person. **Citywalks** (tel. 212/989–2456) offers two-hour walking tours exploring various neighborhoods in depth, weekends at 1 PM for $12. **Urban Explorations** (tel. 718/721–5254)

runs weekend tours with an emphasis on architecture and urban planning; Chinatown is a
specialty. The **Municipal Art Society** (tel. 212/
935–3960) operates a series of bus and walking
tours. The **Museum of the City of New York** (tel.
212/534–1672) sponsors Sunday afternoon walking tours. The **Urban Park Rangers** (tel. 212/
427–4040) offer weekend walks and workshops,
most of them free, in city parks. The **92nd Street
Y** (tel. 212/996–1100) often has something special to offer on weekends and some weekdays.
Other knowledgeable walking-tour guides include **Arthur Gelfand** (tel. 212/222–5343), **Joyce
Gold** (tel. 212/242–5762), and **Arthur Marks** (tel.
212/673–0477).

The most comprehensive listing of tours offered
during a particular week is published in the
"Other Events" section of *New York* magazine's
"Cue" listings.

Self-Guided The **New York Convention and Visitors Bureau's**
Walking Tours "I Love New York Visitors Guide and Map" is
available at the bureau's information center (2
Columbus Circle, tel. 212/397–8222). Walkers in
Brooklyn can pick up two maps—"Brooklyn on
Tour" and "Downtown Brooklyn Walking
Tours"—as well as a handy "Brooklyn Neigh-
borhood Book," all free of charge, at the public
affairs desk of the **Brooklyn Borough Presi-
dent's** office (209 Joralemon St., 3rd floor). All
three are available by mail, at $5 each, from the
Fund for the Borough of Brooklyn (16 Court St.,
Suite 1400 W, Brooklyn, NY 11241, tel. 718/
855–7882).

The **Municipal Art Society of New York** has prepared a comprehensive "Juror's Guide to Lower
Manhattan: Five Walking Tours" for the benefit
of jurors who are often required to kill time
while serving in downtown courthouses. Along
with an explanation of the New York jury system, the pamphlet includes tours of lower Manhattan and Wall Street, the City Hall district,
Chinatown and Little Italy, South Street Seaport, and TriBeCa. Nonjurors can purchase
copies for $5 at **Urban Center Books** (457 Madi-
son Ave. at 51st St., inside the courtyard of the
Helmsley Palace hotel, tel. 212/935–3595).

2 Exploring Manhattan

Orientation

The map of Manhattan bears a Jekyll-and-Hyde aspect. The rational, Dr. Jekyll part prevails above 14th Street, where the streets form a regular grid pattern, imposed in 1811. Consecutively numbered streets run east and west (crosstown), while broad avenues, most of them also numbered, run north (uptown) or south (downtown). The chief exceptions are Broadway (which runs on a diagonal from East 14th to West 79th streets) and the thoroughfares that hug the shores of the Hudson and East rivers.

Fifth Avenue is the east–west dividing line for street addresses: in both directions, they increase in regular increments from there. For example, on 55th Street, the addresses 1–99 East 55th Street run from Fifth, past Madison, to Park (the equivalent of Fourth) avenues, 100–199 East 55th would be between Park and Third avenues, and so on; the addresses 1–99 West 55th Street are between Fifth and Sixth avenues, 100–199 West 55th would be between Sixth and Seventh avenues, and so forth. Above 59th Street, where Central Park interrupts the grid, West Side addresses start numbering at Central Park West, an extension of Eighth Avenue. Avenue addresses are much less regular, for the numbers begin wherever each avenue begins and increase at different increments. An address at 552 Third Avenue, for example, will not necessarily be anywhere near 552 Second Avenue. New Yorkers themselves cannot master the complexities of this system, so in their daily dealings they usually include cross-street references along with avenue addresses (as far as possible, we follow that custom in this book). New Yorkers also rely on the handy Manhattan Address Locator, found in the front of the local phone book.

Below 14th Street—the area that was already settled before the 1811 grid was decreed—Manhattan streets reflect the disordered personality of Mr. Hyde. They may be aligned with the shoreline or they may twist along the route of an ancient cow path. Below 14th Street you'll find West 4th Street intersecting West 11th Street,

Manhattan Neighborhoods

HARLEM
Morningside Park
W. 116th St.
Marcus Garvey Park
E. 116th St.
Randall's Island
Henry Hudson Pkwy.
Broadway
Riverside Drive
Amsterdam Ave.
Columbus Ave.
Central Park West
E. 110th St.
Ward's Island
Central Park
W. 96th St.
E. 96th St.
UPPER WEST SIDE
UPPER EAST SIDE
W. 86th St.
E. 86th St.
West End Ave.
Park Ave.
E. 79th St.
W. 72nd St.
E. 72nd St.
QUEENS
Roosevelt Island
E. 65th St.
Broadway
FDR Dr.
E. 59th St.
Queensboro Bridge
W. 57th St.
5th Ave.
E. 57th St.
11th Ave.
10th Ave.
9th Ave.
8th Ave.
3rd Ave.
1st Ave.
Queens-Midtown Tunnel
W. 42nd St.
MIDTOWN
E. 42nd St.
Ave. of the Americas
Madison Ave.
Lexington Ave.
2nd Ave.
Lincoln Tunnel
W. 34th St.
7th Ave.
Broadway
W. 23rd St.
East River
CHELSEA
E. 23rd St.
GRAMERCY
W. 14th St.
E. 14th St.
GREENWICH VILLAGE
EAST VILLAGE
West St.
W. Houston St.
E. Houston St.
Williamsburg Bridge
N
SOHO
LITTLE ITALY
Canal St.
W. Broadway
CHINA-TOWN
TRIBECA
Manhattan Bridge
Chambers St.
Brooklyn Bridge
Hudson River
LOWER MANHATTAN
BROOKLYN
Battery Park
Brooklyn-Battery Tunnel

Greenwich Street running roughly parallel to Greenwich Avenue, Leroy Street turning into St. Luke's Place for one block and then becoming Leroy again. There's an East Broadway and a West Broadway, both of which run north–south and neither of which is an extension of plain old Broadway. Logic won't help you below 14th Street; only a good street map and good directions will.

Exploring

Tour 1: Rockefeller Center

Numbers in the margin correspond to points of interest on the Midtown map.

When movies and TV shows are set in Manhattan, they often start with a panning shot of Rockefeller Center, for no other city scene—except perhaps the downtown skyline—so clearly says "New York." Begun during the Great Depression of the 1930s by John D. Rockefeller, this 19-building complex occupies nearly 22 acres of prime real estate between Fifth and Seventh avenues and 47th and 52nd streets. Its central cluster of buildings are smooth shafts of warm-hued limestone, streamlined with glistening aluminum, but the real genius of the complex's design was its intelligent use of public space: plazas, concourses, and street-level shops that create a sense of community for the nearly quarter of a million human beings who use it daily. Restaurants, shoe-repair shops, doctors' offices, barbershops, banks, a post office, bookstores, clothing shops, variety stores—all are accommodated within the center, and all parts of the complex are linked by underground passageways.

Rockefeller Center helped turn midtown into New York City's second "downtown" area, which now rivals the Wall Street area in the number of its prestigious tenants. The center itself is a capital of the communications industry, containing the headquarters of a TV network (NBC), several major publishing companies (Time-Warner, McGraw-Hill, and Simon &

Schuster), and the world's largest news-gathering organization, the Associated Press.

Let's begin the tour with a proud symbol of the center's might: the huge statue of Atlas supporting the world that stands sentry before the **International Building** (5th Ave. between 50th and 51st Sts.). The building, with a lobby inspired by ancient Greece and fitted with Grecian marble, houses many foreign consulates, international airlines, and a U. S. passport office.

One block south on Fifth Avenue, between 49th and 50th streets, you'll come to the head of the **Channel Gardens,** a promenade with six pools surrounded by flowerbeds filled with seasonal plantings, conceived by artists, floral designers, and sculptors—10 shows a season. They are called the Channel Gardens because they separate the British building to the north from the French building to the south (above each building's entrance is a coat of arms bearing that country's national symbols). The French building contains among other shops the **Librairie de France,** which sells French-language books, periodicals, and records; its surprisingly large basement contains a Spanish bookstore and a foreign dictionary store.

At the foot of the Channel Gardens is perhaps the most famous sight in Rockefeller Center (if not all of New York): the great gold-leaf statue of the fire-stealing Greek hero **Prometheus,** sprawled on his ledge above the **Lower Plaza.** A quotation from Aeschylus is carved into the red granite wall behind, and 50 jets of water spray around the statue. The plaza's trademark ice-skating rink is open from October through April; the rest of the year, it becomes an open-air café. In December the plaza is decorated with an enormous live Christmas tree. On the Esplanade above the Lower Plaza, flags of the United Nations' members alternate with flags of the states.

The backdrop to the Lower Plaza is the center's tallest tower, the 70-story **GE Building** (formerly the RCA Building until GE acquired RCA in 1986), occupying the block bounded by Rocke-

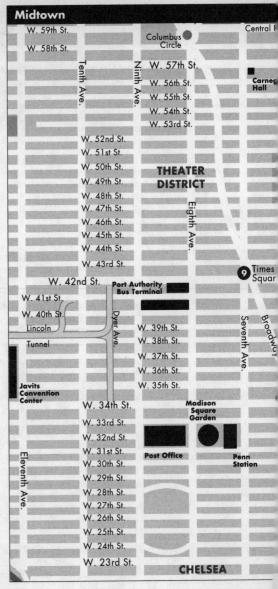

American Craft Museum, **7**
Chrysler Building, **12**
Ford Foundation Building, **13**
GE Building, **3**
Grand Central Terminal, **11**
International Building, **1**
Lower Plaza, **2**
Museum of Modern Art, **6**
Museum of Television and Radio, **5**
New York Public Library, **10**
Radio City Music Hall, **4**
St. Patrick's Cathedral, **8**
Times Square, **9**
United Nations Headquarters, **14**

Midtown

W. 59th St.
W. 58th St.
Tenth Ave.
Ninth Ave.
Columbus Circle
Central F
W. 57th St.
W. 56th St.
W. 55th St.
W. 54th St.
W. 53rd St.
Carneg Hall
W. 52nd St.
W. 51st St.
W. 50th St.
W. 49th St.
THEATER DISTRICT
W. 48th St.
W. 47th St.
W. 46th St.
Eighth Ave.
W. 45th St.
W. 44th St.
W. 43rd St.
9 Times Squar
W. 42nd St.
Port Authority Bus Terminal
W. 41st St.
W. 40th St.
Lincoln
Dyer Ave.
W. 39th St.
W. 38th St.
Seventh Ave.
Broadway
Tunnel
W. 37th St.
W. 36th St.
W. 35th St.
Javits Convention Center
W. 34th St.
Madison Square Garden
W. 33rd St.
W. 32nd St.
W. 31st St.
Eleventh Ave.
W. 30th St.
Post Office
Penn Station
W. 29th St.
W. 28th St.
W. 27th St.
W. 26th St.
W. 25th St.
W. 24th St.
W. 23rd St.
CHELSEA

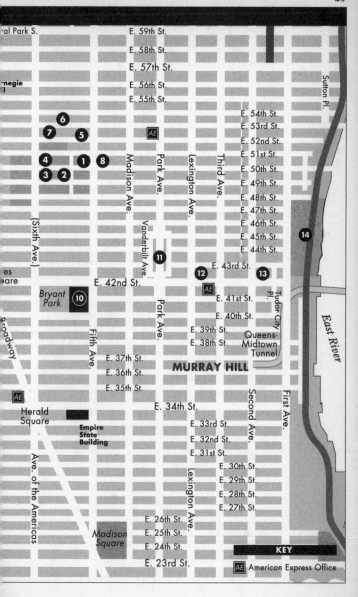

ral Park S.

E. 59th St.

E. 58th St.

E. 57th St.

E. 56th St.

E. 55th St.

E. 54th St.

E. 53rd St.

E. 52nd St.

E. 51st St.

E. 50th St.

E. 49th St.

E. 48th St.

E. 47th St.

E. 46th St.

E. 45th St.

E. 44th St.

E. 43rd St.

E. 42nd St.

E. 41st St.

E. 40th St.

E. 39th St.

E. 38th St.

E. 37th St.

E. 36th St.

E. 35th St.

E. 34th St.

E. 33rd St.

E. 32nd St.

E. 31st St.

E. 30th St.

E. 29th St.

E. 28th St.

E. 27th St.

E. 26th St.

E. 25th St.

E. 24th St.

E. 23rd St.

negie

Sutton Pl.

Madison Ave.

Park Ave.

Lexington Ave.

Third Ave.

Vanderbilt Ave.

[Sixth Ave.]

Fifth Ave.

Park Ave.

Ave. of the Americas

Lexington Ave.

Second Ave.

First Ave.

Tudor City Pl.

Queens-Midtown Tunnel

MURRAY HILL

East River

Bryant Park

Herald Square

Empire State Building

Madison Square

Broadway

es are

KEY

AE American Express Office

feller Plaza, Avenue of the Americas (which New Yorkers call Sixth Avenue), and 49th and 50th streets. The block-long street called Rockefeller Plaza, officially a private street (to maintain that status, it closes to all traffic on one day a year), is often choked with celebrities' black limousines, for this is the headquarters of the NBC television network. From this building emanated some of the first TV programs ever; the "Today" show has been broadcast from here since 1952, and a shot of this building is included in the opening credit sequences of "Saturday Night Live" and "Late Night with David Letterman," both taped here.

One way to see what goes on inside is to spend $7.75 to take a tour of the NBC studios: One leaves from the street level of the GE Building every 15 minutes, 9:30–4:30, Monday–Saturday, and on Sundays during the summer. You can also buy a T-shirt, ashtray, Frisbee, or other paraphernalia bearing the logos of your favorite NBC programs at a boutique in the magnificent black granite lobby.

As you enter the GE Building from Rockefeller Plaza, look up at the striking sculpture of Zeus above the entrance doors, executed in limestone cast in glass by Lee Lawrie, the same artist who sculpted the big Atlas on Fifth Avenue. Inside, crane your neck to see the dramatic ceiling mural by Jose Maria Sert: Wherever you stand, the figure seems to be facing you. From the lobby information desk, go down the escalator in the right-hand corner and turn right to find a detailed exhibit on the history of the center (admission free; open weekdays 9–5). Then wander around the marble catacombs that connect the various components of Rockefeller Center. There's a lot to see: restaurants in all price ranges, from the chic American Festival Cafe to McDonald's; a post office and clean public rest rooms (scarce in midtown); and just about every kind of store. To find your way around, consult the strategically placed directories or obtain the free "Shops and Services Guide" at the GE Building information desk.

Returning to the GE Building lobby, you can take an elevator to the 65th floor to enjoy the spectacular view with drinks or a meal at the **Rainbow Room** (*see* Chapter 4). Exit the GE Building on Sixth Avenue to see the allegorical mosaics above that entrance.

Across 50th Street from the GE Building is America's largest indoor theater, the 6,000-seat ❹ **Radio City Music Hall.** Home of the fabled Rockettes chorus line (which actually started out in St. Louis in 1925), Radio City was built as a movie theater with a stage suitable for live shows as well. Its days as a first-run movie house are long over, but after an announced closing in 1978 Radio City has had an amazing comeback, producing concerts, awards presentations, and special events, along with its own Christmas and Easter extravaganzas. On most days you can take a one-hour tour of the premises. *Tel. 212/247–4777; tour information, 212/ 632–4041. Tour admission: $7 adults, $3.50 children under 6. Tours usually leave from main lobby every 30–45 min, Mon.–Sat. 10:15– 4:45, Sun. 11:15–4:45.*

Later additions to Rockefeller Center include Sixth Avenue's skyscraper triplets—the first between 47th and 48th streets, the second (the **McGraw-Hill Building**), between 48th and 49th streets, and the third between 49th and 50th streets—and their cousin immediately to the north, the **Time & Life Building,** between 50th and 51st streets. All have street-level plazas, but the most interesting is McGraw-Hill's, where a 50-foot steel sun triangle points to the seasonal positions of the sun at noon and a pool demonstrates the relative size of the planets.

Time Out | For supercasual eating when the weather is good, the **Sixth Avenue food vendors** near Rockefeller Center offer the best selection in the city. These "à la cart" diners offer far more than trite hot dogs—there's a truly international menu of tacos, falafel, souvlaki, tempura, Indian curry, Afghani kofta kebabs, or Caribbean beef jerky.

NBC isn't the only network headquartered in Manhattan. The **CBS Building** is a black monolith popularly called Black Rock, on Sixth Avenue between 52nd and 53rd Streets. (ABC, once a close neighbor, has now moved its main office to 66th Street on the West Side.) From here, you can choose among a cluster of museums: The Museum of Television and Radio, the American Craft Museum, or the major collection at the Museum of Modern Art. Go east on 52nd Street

⑤ to the **Museum of Television and Radio,** housed in a new limestone building by Philip Johnson and John Burgee that reminds everyone of a 1930s-vintage radio. Three galleries exhibit photographs and artifacts relating to the history of broadcasting, but most visitors to this museum come to sit at a console and sample its stupendous collection of more than 25,000 TV shows, 10,000 commercials, and 15,000 radio programs. *25 W. 52nd St., tel. 212/621–6800 for daily events or 212/621–6600 for other information. Suggested donation: $5 adults, $4 students, $3 senior citizens and under 13. Open Tues.–Wed. and Fri.–Sun. noon–6, Thurs. noon–8.*

Just east of the Museum of Television and Radio, you'll pass the famous restaurant **The "21" Club,** with its trademark row of jockey statuettes parading along the wrought-iron balcony. Although somewhat declined since its heyday, it still has a burnished men's-club atmosphere and a great downstairs bar. In the movie *The Sweet Smell of Success,* Burt Lancaster as a powerful Broadway columnist held court at his regular table here, besieged by Tony Curtis as a pushy young publicist.

To reach the other museums, on 53rd Street, walk toward Fifth Avenue and turn left to cut through the shopping arcade of 666 Fifth Ave-

⑥ nue. On the north side of 53rd is the **Museum of Modern Art** (MOMA), in a bright and airy six-story structure built around a secluded sculpture garden. In the second- and third-floor galleries of painting and sculpture, some of the world's most famous modern paintings are displayed: Van Gogh's *Starry Night,* Picasso's *Les Demoiselles d'Avignon,* Matisse's *Dance.* The collection also includes photography, architecture, decorative arts, drawings, prints, illustrated books, and films. Afternoon and evening film shows, mostly foreign films and classics, are free with the price of admission; tickets are distributed in the lobby on the day of the performance, and often they go fast. Programs change daily; call 212/708–9480 for a schedule. There's a good bookstore just off the lobby, and the even more interesting MOMA Design Store across the street. And leave time to sit outside in that wonderful Sculpture Garden. *11 W. 53rd St., tel. 212/708–9500. Admission: $7 adults, $4 students and senior citizens, under 16 free. Pay what you wish Thurs. 5–9. Open Fri.–Tues. 11–6, Thurs. 11–9.*

7 On the south side of 53rd, the **American Craft Museum** spotlights the work of contemporary American and international craftspersons working in clay, glass, fabric, wood, metal, or paper. Distinctions between "craft" and "high art" become irrelevant here, for much of this work is provocative and fun to look at. *40 W. 53rd St., tel. 212/956–3535. Admission: $4.50 adults, $2 students and senior citizens, under 13 free. Open Tues. 10–8, Wed.–Sun. 10–5.*

8 Back on Fifth Avenue, at 51st Street, is Gothic-style **St. Patrick's,** the Roman Catholic Cathedral of New York. Dedicated to the patron saint of the Irish—then and now one of New York's principal ethnic groups—the white marble and stone structure was begun in 1858, consecrated in 1879, and completed in 1906. Among the statues in the alcoves around the nave is a striking modern interpretation of the first American-born saint, Mother Elizabeth Seton. From outside, catch one of the city's most photographed views: the ornate white spires of St. Pat's against the black glass curtain of **Olympic Tower,** a multiuse building of shops, offices, and luxury apartments.

Tour 2: Across 42nd Street

Numbers in the margin correspond to points of interest on the Midtown map.

9 While it may not exactly be the Crossroads of the World, as it is often called, **Times Square** is one of New York's principal energy centers. It's one of many New York City "squares" that are actually triangles formed by the angle of Broadway slashing across a major avenue—in this case, crossing Seventh Avenue at 42nd Street. The square itself is occupied by the former

Times Tower, now resheathed in white marble
and called **One Times Square Plaza.** When the
New York Times moved into its new headquarters on December 31, 1904, it publicized the
event with a fireworks show at midnight, thus
starting a New Year's Eve tradition. Each December 31, workmen on this roof lower a 200-
pound ball down the flagpole by hand, just as
they have since 1908. The huge intersection below is mobbed with revelers, and when the ball
hits bottom on the stroke of midnight, pandemonium ensues.

The present headquarters of the *New York
Times* (229 W. 43rd St.) occupies much of the
block between Seventh and Eighth avenues;
look for the blue delivery vans lined up along
43rd Street. From 44th to 51st streets, the cross
streets west of Broadway are lined with some 30
major theaters (*see* Chapter 6). This has been
the city's main theater district since the turn of
the century; movie theaters joined the fray beginning in the 1920s. As the theaters drew
crowds of people in the evenings, advertisers
began to mount huge electric signs here, which
gave the intersection its distinctive nighttime
glitter.

Between 40th and 42nd streets on Fifth Avenue,
you'll find the central research building of the
❿ New York Public Library. This 1911 masterpiece
of Beaux Arts design was financed largely by
John Jacob Astor. Its grand front steps are
guarded by two crouching marble lions—
dubbed "Patience" and "Fortitude" by Mayor
Fiorello La Guardia, who said he visited the facility to "read between the lions." After admir-
ing the white marble neoclassical facade
(crammed with statues, as is typical of Beaux
Arts buildings), walk through the bronze front
doors into the grand marble lobby with its
sweeping double staircase. Turn left and peek
into the Periodicals Room, decorated with
trompe l'oeil paintings by Richard Haas commemorating New York's importance as a publishing center. Then take a (quiet) look upstairs
at the huge, high-ceilinged main reading room, a
haven of scholarly calm, or visit the current exhibition in the art gallery. Among the treasures
you might see are Gilbert Stuart's portrait of

George Washington, Charles Dickens's desk, and Thomas Jefferson's own handwritten copy of the Declaration of Independence. Free one-hour tours, each as individual as the library volunteer who leads it, are given Tuesday–Saturday at 11 AM and 2 PM. *Tel. 212/930–0800. Open Tues.–Wed. 11–7:30, Thurs.–Sat. 10–6.*

⑪ Continue east on 42nd Street to **Grand Central Terminal** (not a "station," as many people call it, since all runs begin or end here). Constructed between 1903 and 1913, this Manhattan landmark was originally designed by a Minnesota architectural firm and later gussied up with Beaux Arts ornamentation. Stop on the south side of 42nd Street to admire the three huge windows separated by columns, and the Beaux Arts clock and sculpture crowning the facade above the elevated roadway (Park Avenue is routed around Grand Central's upper story). Go in the side doors on Vanderbilt Avenue to enter the cavernous main concourse, with its 12-story-high ceiling displaying the constellations of the zodiac. The best time to visit is at rush hour, when this immense room crackles with the frenzy of scurrying commuters, dashing every which way. *Free tours Wed. at 12:30 PM (meet in front of Chemical Bank inside terminal on main level), tel. 212/935–3960.*

Ask New Yorkers to name their favorite skyscraper and most will choose the Art Deco **⑫** **Chrysler Building** at 42nd Street and Lexington Avenue. Although the Chrysler Corporation itself moved out a long time ago, this graceful shaft culminating in a stainless-steel spire still captivates the eye and the imagination. The building has no observation deck, but you can go inside its elegant dark lobby, which is faced with African marble and covered with a ceiling mural that salutes transportation and human endeavor.

⑬ The **Ford Foundation Building** (320 E. 43rd St., with an entrance on 42nd St.) encloses a 12-story, ⅓-acre greenhouse. With a terraced garden, a still pool, and a couple of dozen full-grown trees as centerpieces, the Ford garden is open to the public—for tranquil strolling, not for picnics—weekdays from 9 to 5.

Climb the steps along 42nd Street between First and Second avenues to enter **Tudor City,** a self-contained complex of a dozen buildings featuring half-timbering and lots of stained glass. Constructed between 1925 and 1928, two of the apartment buildings of this residential enclave originally had no east-side windows, lest the tenants be forced to gaze at the slaughterhouses, breweries, and glue factories then located along the East River. Today, however, they're missing a wonderful view of the United Nations Headquarters; you'll have to walk to the terrace at the end of 43rd Street to overlook the UN. This will place you at the head of the **Sharansky Steps** (named for Natan—formerly Anatoly—Sharansky, the Soviet dissident), which run along the **Isaiah Wall** (inscribed "They Shall Beat Their Swords Into Plowshares"); you'll also look down into **Ralph J. Bunche Park** (named for the black American UN undersecretary) and **Raoul Wallenberg Walk** (named for the Swedish diplomat and World War II hero).

⑭ The **United Nations Headquarters** complex occupies a lushly landscaped 18-acre riverside tract just east of First Avenue between 42nd and 48th streets. Its rose garden is especially pleasant to stroll in, although picnicking is strictly forbidden. A line of flagpoles with banners representing the current roster of 159 member nations stands before the striking 550-foot-high slab of the Secretariat Building, with the domed General Assembly Building nestled at its side. The headquarters were designed in 1947–53 by an international team of architects led by Wallace Harrison. You can enter the General Assembly Building at the 46th Street door; the interior corridors overflow with imaginatively diverse artwork donated by member nations. Free tickets to most sessions are available on a first-come, first-served basis 15 minutes before sessions begin; pick them up in the General Assembly lobby. (The full General Assembly is in session from the third Tuesday in September to the end of December.) Visitors can take early luncheon in the Delegates Dining Room (jacket required for men) or eat anytime in the public coffee shop. *Tel. 212/963–7713. Tours offered* *daily 9:15–4:45. 1-hr tours leave the General Assembly lobby every 15–20 min. Tour admission: $6.50 adults, $4.50 students and senior citizens, $3.50 students in 9th grade and under. Children under 5 not permitted.*

Tour 3: Museum Mile

Numbers in the margin correspond to points of interest on the Museum Mile and Central Park map.

Once known as Millionaire's Row, the stretch of Fifth Avenue between 79th and 104th streets has been fittingly renamed Museum Mile, for it now contains an impressive cluster of cultural institutions. The connection is more than coincidental: Many museums are housed in what used to be the great mansions of merchant princes and wealthy industrialists. In 1979 a group of 10 Fifth Avenue institutions formed a consortium that, among other activities, sponsors a Museum Mile Festival each June. The Frick Collection and the Whitney Museum of American Art are not officially part of the Museum Mile Consortium, but they're located close enough to be added to this tour.

It would be impossible to do justice to all these collections in one outing; the Metropolitan Museum alone contains too much to see in a day. You may want to select one or two museums to linger in and simply walk past the others, appreciating their exteriors (this in itself constitutes a minicourse in modern architecture). Save the rest for another day—or for your next trip to New York.

Be sure to pick the right day of the week for this tour: Most of these museums are closed on Mondays, but some have free admission during extended hours on Tuesday evenings.

● Begin at Fifth Avenue and 70th Street with **The Frick Collection,** housed in an ornate, imposing Beaux Arts mansion built in 1914 for coke-and-steel baron Henry Clay Frick, who wanted the superb art collection he was amassing to be kept far from the soot and smoke of Pittsburgh, where he'd made his fortune. Strolling through the mansion, one can imagine how it felt to live

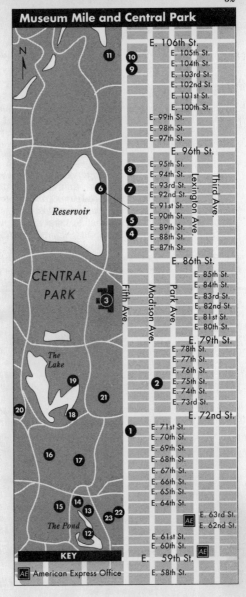

Arsenal, **22**
Bethesda
Fountain, **18**
Carousel, **15**
Central Park
Zoo, **23**
Conservatory
Garden, **11**
Conservatory
Water, **21**
Cooper-Hewitt
Museum, **6**
The Dairy, **14**
El Museo del
Barrio, **10**
Frick
Collection, **1**
Guggenheim
Museum, **4**
International
Center of
Photography, **8**
Jewish
Museum, **7**
Loeb
Boathouse, **19**
The Mall, **17**
Metropolitan
Museum of
Art, **3**
Museum of the
City of New
York, **9**
National
Academy of
Design, **5**
The Pond, **12**
Sheep
Meadow, **16**
Strawberry
Fields, **20**
Whitney
Museum, **2**
Wollman
Rink, **13**

with Vermeers by the front stairs, Gainsborough and Reynolds portraits in the dining room, canvases by Constable and Turner in the library, and Titians, Holbeins, a Giovanni Bellini, and an El Greco in the living room. Some of the collection's best pieces include Rembrandt's *The Polish Rider* and Jean-Honoré Fragonard's series *The Progress of Love*. Even the resting area is a masterpiece: a tranquil indoor court with a fountain and glass ceiling. *1 E. 70th St., tel. 212/ 288–0700. Admission: $3 adults, $1.50 students and senior citizens. Children under 10 not admitted. Open Tues.–Sat. 10–6, Sun. 1–6, closed holidays.*

❷ Walk one block east to Madison Avenue and head up to 75th Street to **The Whitney Museum of American Art.** This museum grew out of a gallery in the studio of the sculptor and collector Gertrude Vanderbilt Whitney, whose talent and taste were fortuitously accompanied by the wealth of two prominent families. The current building, opened in 1966, is a minimalist gray granite vault, separated from Madison Avenue by a dry moat; it was designed by Marcel Breuer, a member of the Bauhaus school, which prized functionality in architecture. The monolithic exterior is much more forbidding than the interior, where changing exhibitions offer an intelligent survey of 20th-century American works; a third-floor gallery features a sample of the permanent collection, including Edward Hopper's haunting *Early Sunday Morning* (1930), Georgia O'Keeffe's *White Calico Flower* (1931), and Jasper Johns's *Three Flags* (1958). Alexander Calder's *Circus*, a playful construction he tinkered with throughout his life (1898–1976), stands near the front entrance. *945 Madison Ave. at 75th St., tel. 212/570– 3676. Admission: $5 adults, $3 senior citizens; free for students with valid ID and children under 12. Open Wed. and Fri.–Sun. 11–6, Thurs. 1–8.*

❸ **The Metropolitan Museum of Art** has valid evidence for billing itself as "New York's number-one tourist attraction"; certainly the quality and range of its holdings make it one of the world's greatest museums. It's the largest art museum in the Western Hemisphere (1.6 million square feet), and its permanent collection of more than 3 million works of art from all over the world includes objects from prehistoric to modern times. The museum, founded in 1870, moved to this location in 1880, but the original redbrick building by Calvert Vaux has since been encased in other architecture. The majestic Fifth Avenue facade, designed by Richard Morris Hunt, was built in 1902 of gray Indiana limestone; later additions eventually surrounded the original building on the sides and back. (On a side wall of the new ground-floor European Sculpture Court, you can glimpse the museum's original redbrick facade.)

The Fifth Avenue entrance leads into the Great Hall, a soaring neoclassical chamber that has been designated a landmark in its own right. Past the admission booths, a vast marble staircase leads up to the European painting galleries, whose highlights include Botticelli's *The Last Communion of St. Jerome*, Pieter Brueghel's *The Harvesters*, El Greco's *View of Toledo*, Johannes Vermeer's *Young Woman with a Water Jug*, and Rembrandt's *Aristotle with a Bust of Homer*.

American art has its own wing, back in the northwest corner; the best approach is on the first floor, where you enter through a refreshingly light and airy garden court graced with Tiffany stained-glass windows, cast-iron staircases by Louis Sullivan, and a marble Federal-style facade taken from the Wall Street branch of the United States Bank.

There is much more to the Met than paintings, however. Visitors with a taste for classical art should go immediately to the left of the Great Hall on the first floor to see the Greek and Roman statuary, not to mention a large collection of rare Roman wall paintings excavated from the lava of Mount Vesuvius. Directly above these galleries, on the second floor, you'll find room after room of Grecian urns and other classical vases. The Met's awesome Egyptian collection, spanning some 3,000 years, lies on the first floor directly to the right of the Great Hall. Its centerpiece is the Temple of Dendur, an entire Roman-period temple (circa 15 BC) donated by the Egyptian government in thanks for U.S. help in saving ancient monuments.

Although it exhibits only a portion of its vast holdings, the Met offers more than can reasonably be seen in one visit. Be aware also that cuts in cultural funding have forced the museum to close certain galleries either mornings or afternoons Tuesday–Thursday; in the course of a day, you can still see anything you want, but ask at the desk for an alternating-gallery schedule to avoid frustration. Choose what you want to see, find a map, and plan your tour accordingly. Walking tours and lectures are free with your admission contribution. Tours covering various sections of the museum begin about every 15 minutes on weekdays, less frequently on weekends; they depart from the Tour Board in the Great Hall. Self-guided audio tours can also be rented at a desk in the Great Hall. Lectures, often related to temporary exhibitions, are given frequently. *5th Ave. at 82nd St., tel. 212/535-7710. Suggested contribution: $6 adults, $3 students and senior citizens, children under 13 free. Open Tues.–Thurs. and Sun. 9:30–5:15, Fri. and Sat. 9:30–8:45.*

Time Out While the Metropolitan has a good museum café, only a block away is a friendly, sparkling-clean coffee shop: **Nectar of 82nd** (1090 Madison Ave. at 82nd St., tel. 212/772–0916). Omelets, salads, soups, burgers—the portions are generous and the prices quite reasonable. Expect a short wait at weekend lunch, but the crowd moves quickly, though no one ever feels rushed.

❹ Frank Lloyd Wright's **Guggenheim Museum** (opened in 1959) is a controversial work of architecture—even many of those who like its assertive six-story spiral rotunda will admit that it does not result in the best space in which to view art. Inside, under a 92-foot-high glass dome, a quarter-mile-long ramp spirals down past changing exhibitions of modern art. A new annex opened in June 1992, creating expanded gallery space to display the newly acquired Panza Collection of Minimalist art, among other works. The museum has especially strong holdings in Wassily Kandinsky, Paul Klee, and Pablo

Picasso; the oldest pieces are by the French Impressionists. *1071 5th Ave. at 89th St., tel. 212/423-3500. Admission: $7 adults, $4 students and senior citizens, children under 12 free. Open Fri.-Wed. 10-8.*

⑤ A block north is **The National Academy of Design,** housed in a stately 19th-century mansion and a pair of town houses on 89th Street. The academy itself, which was founded in 1825, required each elected member to donate a representative work of art, which has resulted in a strong collection of 19th- and 20th-century American art. (Members have included Samuel F. B. Morse, Winslow Homer, John Singer Sargent, Frank Lloyd Wright, and Robert Rauschenberg.) *1083 5th Ave. at 89th St., tel. 212/369-4880. Admission: $3.50 adults, $2 senior citizens and children under 16; free Tues. 5-8. Open Tues. noon-8, Wed.-Sun. noon-5.*

At 91st Street you'll find the former residence of industrialist Andrew Carnegie, now the home of **⑥** the **Cooper-Hewitt Museum** (officially the Smithsonian Institution's National Museum of Design). Carnegie sought comfort more than show when he built this 64-room house on what was the outskirts of town in 1901; he administered his extensive philanthropic projects from the first-floor study. (Note the low doorways—Carnegie was only five feet two inches tall.) The core of the museum's collection was begun in 1897 by the three Hewitt sisters, granddaughters of inventor and industrialist Peter Cooper; major holdings include drawings, prints, textiles, furniture, metalwork, ceramics, glass, woodwork, and wall coverings. *2 E. 91st St., tel. 212/860-6868. Admission: $3 adults, $1.50 students and senior citizens, children under 12 free; free to all Tues. 5-9. Open Tues. 10-9, Wed.-Sat. 10-5, Sun. noon-5.*

Time Out **Jackson Hole** (Madison Ave. and 91st St.) is a cheerful spot that serves the great American hamburger plus other sandwiches, omelets, chicken, and salads. Ski posters evoke the mood of the eponymous Wyoming resort. Prices are reasonable; beer is available.

● **The Jewish Museum** (1109 5th Ave. at 92nd St., tel. 212/399–3430), set in a gray stone Gothic-style château built in 1908, owns the largest collection of Jewish ceremonial objects in the Western Hemisphere. The museum was closed for renovation until early 1993, during which time it held exhibitions at the New-York Historical Society (77th St. and Central Park West, tel. 212/399–3344; *see* Tour 5, *below*). Once it moves back to Fifth Avenue, it will be open Sunday–Thursday, with late hours on Tuesday, but exact hours and admission prices had not been set at press time.

The handsome, well-proportioned Georgian-style mansion on the corner of Fifth Avenue and 94th Street was built in 1914 for Willard Straight, founder of *The New Republic* maga-
● zine. Today it is the home of **The International Center of Photography** (ICP), a relatively young institution—founded in 1974—building a strong collection of 20th-century photography. Its changing exhibitions often focus on the work of a single prominent photographer or one photographic genre (portraits, architecture, etc.). The bookstore carries an impressive array of photography-oriented books, prints, and postcards. *1130 5th Ave. at 94th St., tel. 212/860–1777. Admission: $3.50 adults, $2 students and senior citizens, $1 children under 12. Open Tues. 11–8, Wed.–Sun. 11–6.*

● **The Museum of the City of New York** traces the course of Big Apple history, from the Dutch settlers of Nieuw Amsterdam to the present day, with period rooms, dioramas, slide shows, and clever displays of memorabilia. An exhibit on the Port of New York illuminates the role of the harbor in New York's rise to greatness; the noteworthy Toy Gallery has several meticulously detailed dollhouses. Weekend programs appeal especially to children. *5th Ave. at 103rd St., tel. 212/534–1672. Suggested contribution: $5 adults; $3 students, senior citizens, and children; $8 family. Open Wed.–Sat. 10–5, Sun. and all legal holidays (not Mon.) 1–5.*

● **El Museo Del Barrio,** founded in 1969, concentrates on Latin culture in general, with a particular emphasis on Puerto Rican art. ("El Barrio" means "the neighborhood," and the museum is positioned on the edge of Spanish Harlem.) The permanent collection includes numerous pre-Columbian artifacts. *1230 5th Ave. at 104th St., tel. 212/831–7272. Suggested contribution: $2. Open Wed.–Sun. 11–5.*

Having completed this long walk, you may want to reward yourself by crossing the street to Central Park's **Conservatory Garden.** The entrance, at 105th Street, is through elaborate wrought-iron gates that once graced the mansion of Cornelius Vanderbilt II. In contrast to the deliberately rustic effect of the rest of the park, this is a symmetrical, formal garden. The central lawn is bordered by yew hedges and flowering crab apple trees, leading to a reflecting pool flanked by a large wisteria arbor. To the south is a high-hedged flower garden named after Frances Hodgson Burnett, author of the children's classic *The Secret Garden.* To the north is the Untermeyer Fountain, with its three spirited girls dancing at the heart of a huge circular bed where 20,000 tulips bloom in the spring, and 5,000 chrysanthemums in the fall.

Tour 4: Central Park

Numbers in the margin correspond to points of interest on the Museum Mile and Central Park map.

It's amazing that 843 acres of the world's most valuable real estate should be set aside as a park, yet the city's 1856 decision to do so has proved to be marvelous wisdom, for Central Park contributes mightily toward helping New Yorkers maintain their sanity. It provides space large enough to get lost in (the entire principality of Monaco would fit within its borders), space where you can escape from the rumble of traffic to hear a bird sing or watch an earthworm tumble through the soil.

Although it appears to be simply a swath of rolling countryside exempted from urban development, Central Park is in fact one of the most cunningly planned artificial landscapes ever built. When they began in 1858, designers Frederick Law Olmsted and Calvert Vaux were presented with a swampy neighborhood of a few farms, houses, and a church. It took them 16 years, $14 million, and 5 million cubic yards of moved earth to create this playground of lush lawns, thick forests, and quiet ponds. Hills and tunnels artfully conceal transverse roads (65th, 79th, 86th, and 97th streets) so crosstown traffic will not disturb park goers, and a meandering circular drive carries vehicular traffic in the park (the drive is closed to auto traffic on weekends year-round).

To explore the park on foot, begin at Grand Army Plaza (Fifth Avenue and 59th Street). Enter the park along the main road (East Drive), turning down the first path to your left to the **12** **Pond.** Walk along the shore to the Gapstow Bridge (each of the park's 30 bridges has its own name and individual design), where you can look back at the often-photographed view of midtown skyscrapers reflected in the pond. From left to right, you'll see the peak-roofed brown Sherry-Netherland hotel, the black-and-white General Motors building, the rose-colored "Chippendale" top of the AT&T building, the black glass shaft of Trump Tower, and in front the green gables of the white Plaza Hotel.

Return to the main path and continue north to **13** **Wollman Memorial Rink,** a skating rink that has become a symbol of municipal inefficiency to New Yorkers. Fruitless and costly attempts by the city to repair the deteriorated facility had kept it closed for years, until builder Donald Trump adopted the project and quickly completed it. Even if you don't want to join in, you can stand on the terrace here to watch the skaters—ice-skating throughout the winter, roller-skating and miniature golf April to October. The blaring loudspeaker system in this otherwise quiet park makes the rink hard to ignore. *Tel. 212/517–4800. Admission: $5 adults, $2.50 children under 13. Skate rental: $2.70. Open Mon. 10–5, Tues.–Thurs. 10–9:30, Fri. and Sat. 10 AM–11 PM, Sun. 10–9:30.*

From April to October part of the rink becomes the **Gotham Miniature Golf** course, where putters maneuver around scale models of various city landmarks. *Tel. 212/517–4800. Admission: $6.50 adults, $3.50 children under age 13. Open*

Mon. 10–5, Tues.–Thurs. 10–9:30, Fri. and Sat. 10 AM–11 PM, Sun. 10–9:30.

⑭ Turn your back to the rink and you'll see the painted, pointed eaves, steeple, and high-pitched slate roof of the **Dairy,** originally an actual dairy built in the 19th century when cows grazed here. Today it's the park's Visitor Center, offering maps, souvenirs, videos, children's programs, and some very interesting hands-on exhibits. *Tel. 212/794–6565. Open Tues.–Sun. 11–4, Fri. 1–4.*

⑮ As you leave the Dairy, follow the path to your right (west) and under the Playmates Arch—aptly named, because it leads to a large area of ballfields and playgrounds. Coming through the arch, you'll hear the jaunty music of the **Carousel.** Although this isn't the park's original one, it was built in 1908 and later moved here from Coney Island. Its 58 ornately hand-carved steeds are three-quarters the size of real horses, and the organ plays a variety of tunes, new and old. *Tel. 212/879–0244. Admission: 90¢. Open summer, weekdays 10:30–5:30, weekends 10:30–6:30; winter, daily 10:30–4:30, weather permitting.*

⑯ Climb the slope to the left of the Playmates Arch and walk beside the Center Drive. From here you can choose between two parallel routes: Turn left onto the paved path that runs alongside the chain-link fence of the **Sheep Meadow,** or go all the way to the circular garden **⑰** at the foot of the **Mall.** The broad formal walkway of the Mall called **"The Literary Walk"** is a peaceful spot, lined with the largest group of American elms in the northeast and statues of famous men, including Shakespeare, Robert Burns, and Sir Walter Scott. The other path, however, buzzes on weekends with human activity: volleyball games, roller-skating, impromptu music fests. By contrast, the 15 grassy acres of the Sheep Meadow make an ideal spot for picnicking or sunbathing. It's an officially designated quiet zone, where the most vigorous sports allowed are kite-flying and Frisbee-tossing. This lawn was actually used for grazing sheep until 1934; the nearby sheepfold was turned into the Tavern on the Green restaurant (*see* Tour 5, *below*).

The 72nd Street transverse—the only crosstown street that connects with the East, Center, and West drives—cuts across the park just north of here, but you can cross it or pass beneath it through a lovely tiled arcade to reach **18** **Bethesda Fountain,** set on an elaborately patterned paved terrace on the edge of the **Lake.** This ornate, three-tiered fountain is named after the biblical Bethesda pool in Jerusalem, which was supposedly given healing powers by an angel (hence the angel rising from the center). Perch on the low terrace wall or the edge of the fountain and watch the rowboaters stroke past on the lake. If you want to get out on the water yourself, take the path east from the terrace to **Loeb Boathouse,** where in season you can **19** rent a rowboat. The boathouse also operates a bike-rental facility and a better-than-average restaurant. *Boat rental $7 per hr, $20 deposit; tel. 212/517–4723. Bicycle rental $6 per hr, tandems $12 per hr; tel. 212/861–4137. Open daily 11–6, May–Oct..*

Head west on the 72nd Street transverse; on the rocky outcrop directly across the road, you'll see a statue of a falconer gracefully lofting his bird. Turn to the right and you'll see a more prosaic statue, a pompous bronze figure of Daniel Webster with his hand thrust into his coat. Cross the drive behind Webster, being careful to watch for bikes hurtling around the curve.

20 You've now come to **Strawberry Fields,** the "international peace garden" memorializing singer John Lennon. Climbing up a hill, its curving paths, shrubs, trees, and flower beds create a deliberately informal pastoral landscape, reminiscent of the English parks Lennon may have been thinking of when he wrote the Beatles song "Strawberry Fields." A black-and-white mosaic set into one of the sidewalks contains simply the word "Imagine," another Lennon song title. Just beyond the trees, at 72nd Street and Central Park West, is the Dakota (*see* Tour 5, *below*), where Lennon and his wife, Yoko Ono, lived at the time of his death in 1980.

Head back east on the 72nd Street drive to one
of the park's most formal areas: the symmetrical
(21) stone basin of the **Conservatory Water,** where
you can watch some very sophisticated model
boats being raced each Saturday morning at 10.
(Unfortunately, model boats are not for rent
here.) At the north end of the pond is one of the
park's most beloved statues, José de Creeft's
1960 bronze sculpture of **Alice in Wonderland,**
sitting on a giant mushroom with the Mad Hat-
ter, White Rabbit, and leering Cheshire Cat in
attendance. Children are encouraged to clam-
ber all over it. On the west side of the pond, a
bronze statue of **Hans Christian Andersen,** the
Ugly Duckling at his feet, is the site of storytell-
ing hours on summer weekends.

Climb the hill at the far end of the Conservatory
Water, cross the 72nd Street transverse, and
follow the path south to the Children's Zoo, oft-
threatened by city budget cuts and currently
closed pending reconstruction. Pass under the
Denesmouth Arch to the **Delacorte Clock,** a delightful glockenspiel set above a redbrick arch.
Every hour its six-animal band circles around
and plays a tune, while monkeys on the top ham-
mer their bells. A path to the left will take you
(22) around to the front entrance of the **Arsenal,** the
Parks Department's headquarters, occupying
what was a pre–Civil War arsenal. Since the city
acquired it in 1857, it has served as, among other
things, the first home of the American Museum
of Natural History, now on Central Park West at
79th Street (*see* Tour 5, *below*). The downstairs
lobby has some great murals; an upstairs gallery features changing exhibtions, often of
great interest to kids. *Tel. 212/360–8163. Open
weekdays 9:30–4:30.*

(23) Just past the clock is the **Central Park Zoo,** a
small but delightful menagerie. Clustered
around the central Sea Lion Pool are separate
exhibits for each of the Earth's major environ-
ments; the Polar Circle features a huge penguin
tank and polar-bear floe; the open-air Temper-
ate Territory is highlighted by a pit of chatter-
ing monkeys; and the Tropic Zone contains the
flora and fauna of a miniature rain forest. This is
a good zoo for children and adults who like to
take time to watch the animals; even a leisurely

visit will take only about an hour, for there are only about 100 species on display. Go to the Bronx Zoo (*see* Other Attractions, *below*) if you need tigers, giraffes, and elephants—the biggest specimens here are the polar bears. *Tel. 212/439-6500. Admission: $2.50 adults, $1.25 senior citizens, 50¢ children 3-12. No children under 16 allowed in without adult. Open Apr.-Oct., Mon. and Wed.-Fri. 10-4:30, Tues. 10-7, weekends and holidays 10-5; Nov.-Mar., daily 10-4.*

Tour 5: The Upper West Side

Numbers in the margin correspond to points of interest on the Upper West Side map.

The Upper West Side has never been as fashionable as the East Side, despite the fact that it has a similar mix of real estate—large apartment buildings along Central Park West, West End Avenue, and Riverside Drive; and town houses on the shady, quiet cross streets. Once a haven for the Jewish intelligentsia, by the 1960s the West Side had become a rather grungy multi-ethnic community. In the 1970s gentrification began slowly, with actors, writers, and gays as the earliest settlers. Today, however, this area is quite desirable, with lots of restored brownstones and high-priced co-op apartments.

When you pass **The Ballet Shop** (1887 Broadway, between 61st and 62nd Sts.), a mecca for balletomanes, you'll know you're getting close to New York's major site for the performing
1 arts: **Lincoln Center,** covering an eight-block area west of Broadway between 62nd and 66th streets. This unified complex of pale travertine marble was built during the 1960s to supplant an urban ghetto (*West Side Story* was filmed on the slum's gritty, deserted streets just before the demolition crews moved in). Lincoln Center can seat nearly 18,000 spectators at one time in its various halls (*see* Chapter 6).

Stand on Broadway, facing the central court with its huge fountain, which Mel Brooks fans may recognize as the spot where Zero Mostel and Gene Wilder danced exuberantly in *The Producers.* The three concert halls on this plaza clearly relate to each other architecturally, with

American
Museum of
Natural
History, **5**

Barnard
College, **8**

Cathedral of St.
John the
Divine, **6**

Columbia
University, **7**

The Dakota, **3**

Grant's Tomb, **9**

Hayden
Planetarium, **5**

Lincoln
Center, **1**

Museum of
American Folk
Art, **2**

New-York
Historical
Society, **4**

Riverside
Church, **10**

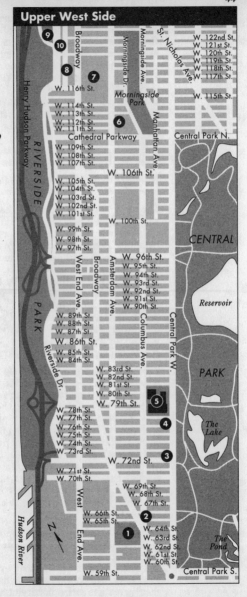

Upper West Side

their symmetrical bi-level facades, yet each has slightly different lines and different details. To your left, huge honeycomb lights hang on the portico of the **New York State Theater,** home to the New York City Ballet and the New York City Opera. Straight ahead, at the rear of the plaza, is the **Metropolitan Opera House,** its brilliant-colored Chagall tapestries visible through the arched lobby windows; the Metropolitan Opera and American Ballet Theatre perform here. To your right, abstract bronze sculptures distinguish **Avery Fisher Hall,** host to the New York Philharmonic Orchestra.

Wander through the plaza, then angle to your left between the New York State Theater and the Metropolitan Opera House into **Damrosch Park,** where summer open-air festivals are often accompanied by free concerts at the **Guggenheim Bandshell.** Angle to your right from the plaza, between the Metropolitan and Avery Fisher, and you'll come to the North Plaza, with a massive Henry Moore sculpture reclining in a reflecting pool. To the rear is the **Library and Museum of the Performing Arts,** a branch of the New York Public Library with an extensive collection of books, records, and scores on music, theater, and dance; visitors can listen to any of 42,000 records and tapes, or check out its four galleries. Next to the library is the wide glass-walled lobby of the **Vivian Beaumont** and **Mitzi E. Newhouse theaters,** officially considered Broadway houses although far removed from the theater district.

An overpass leads from this plaza across 65th Street to the world-renowned **Juilliard School** (for music and theater). Turn right for an elevator down to street level and **Alice Tully Hall,** home of the Chamber Music Society of Lincoln Center and the New York Film Festival. Or turn left from the overpass and follow the walkway west to Lincoln Center's newest arts venue, the **Walter Reade Theater,** opened in the fall of 1991, showing five "non-Hollywood"-style films a day, seven days a week.

Visitors can wander freely through the lobbies of all these buildings. A one-hour guided "Introduction to Lincoln Center" tour covers the center's history and wealth of artworks, and usually visits the three principal theaters, performance schedules permitting. *Tel. 212/875–5351 for schedule and reservations. Admission: $7.50 adults, $6.50 students and senior citizens, $4.25 children 6–12.*

Across the busy intersection, the long-orphaned **②** **Museum of American Folk Art** has found a new home at Columbus Avenue and 66th Street. (This gallery will become an annex once the museum's permanent headquarters on West 53rd Street are completed in 1994.) Its collection includes naïve paintings, quilts, carvings, dolls, trade signs, painted wood carousel horses, and a giant Indian-chief copper weathervane. *2 Lincoln Sq., tel. 212/977–7298. Suggested donation: $2. Open Tues.–Sun. 11:30–7:30.*

Around the corner on 66th Street is the headquarters of the ABC television network; ABC owns several buildings along Columbus Avenue as well, including some studios where news shows and soap operas are filmed, so keep an eye out for stars.

Turn onto West 67th Street and head toward Central Park along one of the city's most handsome blocks. Many of the apartment buildings here were designed as "studio buildings," with immense windows that make them ideal for artists; look up at the facades and imagine the high-ceilinged spaces within. Also notice the Gothic motifs, carved in white stone or wrought in iron, that decorate several of these buildings at street level. Perhaps the finest apartment building on the block is the **Hotel des Artistes** (1 W. 67th St.), built in 1918, with its elaborate mock-Elizabethan lobby. Its tenants have included Isadora Duncan, Rudolph Valentino, Norman Rockwell, Noël Coward, Fannie Hurst, and contemporary actors Joel Grey and Richard Thomas; another tenant, Howard Chandler Christy, designed the lush, soft-toned murals in the excellent ground-floor restaurant, **Café des Artistes** (*see* Chapter 4), where Louis Malle's *My Dinner with André* was filmed.

Another dining landmark is just inside Central Park at 66th Street, **Tavern on the Green** (*see*

Chapter 4). Originally built as a sheepfold, in the days when sheep grazed on the meadows of the park, it was converted into a restaurant in the 1930s. Many of its dining rooms have fine park views, and at night white lights strung through the surrounding trees create an undeniably magical effect.

3 Continue up Central Park West to 72nd Street, where the stately **Dakota** presides over the northwest corner. Its tenants have included Boris Karloff, Judy Holliday, José Ferrer and Rosemary Clooney, Lauren Bacall, Rex Reed, and Gilda Radner. Resembling a buff-colored castle, with copper turrets, its slightly spooky appearance was played up in the movie *Rosemary's Baby*, which was filmed here. Stop by the gate on 72nd Street; this is the spot where, in December 1980, a deranged fan shot John Lennon as he came home from a recording session. Lennon is memorialized in Central Park's Strawberry Fields, across the street (*see* Tour 4, *above*).

Proceed up Central Park West and you'll see several other famous apartment buildings, including **The Langham** (135 Central Park West), where Mia Farrow's apartment was featured in Woody Allen's film *Hannah and Her Sisters;* the twin-towered **San Remo** (145-146 Central Park West), over the years home to Rita Hayworth, Dustin Hoffman, Raquel Welch, Paul Simon, Tony Randall, and Diane Keaton—but not to Madonna, whose application was rejected because of her flamboyant lifestyle; and **The Kenilworth** (151 Central Park West), with its immense ornate pair of front columns, once home to Basil Rathbone, film's quintessential Sherlock Holmes.

4 The city's oldest museum, **The New-York Historical Society,** preserves within its stern gray granite home what was unique about the city's past, including the quaint hyphen in "New-York." Along with changing exhibits of American history and art, the museum displays Audubon watercolors, early toys, Tiffany lamps, antique vehicles, and Hudson River School landscapes. *170 Central Park West and 77th St., tel. 212/873-3400. Admission: $4.50 adults, $3 sen-*

ior citizens, $1 children under 12; pay what you wish Tues. Open Tues., Wed., Fri., and Sun. 11–5; Thurs. 11–8.

5 The **American Museum of Natural History,** the attached **Hayden Planetarium,** and their surrounding grounds occupy a four-block tract bounded by Central Park West, Columbus Avenue, and 77th and 81st streets. As you approach at 77th Street, you can see the original architecture in the pink granite corner towers, with their beehive crowns. A more classical facade was added along Central Park West, with its centerpiece an enormous equestrian statue of President Theodore Roosevelt, naturalist and explorer.

With a collection of more than 36 million artifacts, the museum displays something for every taste, from a 94-foot blue whale to the 563-carat Star of India sapphire. Among the most enduringly popular exhibits are the wondrously detailed dioramas of animal habitat groups, on the first and second floors just behind the rotunda, and the fourth-floor halls full of dinosaur skeletons (some galleries will be closed for renovations). A five-story-tall cast of *Barosaurus* rears on its hind legs in the Roosevelt Rotunda, protecting its fossilized baby from a fossil allosaur. The Naturemax Theater projects films on a giant screen; the Hayden Planetarium (on 81st Street) has two stories of exhibits, plus several different Sky Shows projected on 22 wraparound screens; its rock-music Laser Shows draw crowds of teenagers on Friday and Saturday nights. *Museum: tel. 212/769–5100. Suggested contribution: $5 adults, $2.50 children. Open Sun.–Thurs. 10–5:45; Fri.–Sat. 10–8:45. Planetarium: tel. 212/769–5920. Admission: $5 adults, $3.75 senior citizens and students; $2.50 children 2–12; $7 for laser show. Open weekdays 12:30–4:45, Sat. 10–5:45, Sun. noon–5:45. Naturemax Theater film admission: $5 adults, $3.75 senior citizens and students, $2.50 children. Call 212/769–5650 for show times.*

Time Out For a delicious lunch of pizza or pasta, stop by **Presto's** (434 Amsterdam Ave. at 81st St., tel. 212/721–9141), a casual neighborhood restau-

rant where kids are welcome. The carrot cake is
a good bet for dessert.

6 Take a cab or the Amsterdam Avenue bus uptown to 112th Street and the **Cathedral of St.
John the Divine,** New York's major Episcopal
church and, when completed, to be the largest
cathedral in the world (St. Peter's of Rome is
larger, but it's technically a basilica). Here you
can have a rare, fascinating look at a Gothic cathedral in progress. Its first cornerstone was
laid in 1892 and a second in 1925, but with the
U.S. entry into World War II, construction
came to a "temporary" halt that lasted until
1982. St. John's follows traditional Gothic en-
gineering—it is supported by stonemasonry
rather than by a steel skeleton—so new stone-
cutters, many of them youngsters from nearby
Harlem neighborhoods, had to be trained before
the current work could proceed on the two front
towers, the transept, and, finally, the great central tower. A model in the superb gift shop inside shows what the cathedral might look like
when completed, probably quite a few years into
the future.

The cathedral's vast nave, the length of two
football fields, can seat 5,000 worshipers. The
second chapel to your left is the only **Poet's Corner** in the United States. The **Baptistry,** to the
left of the altar, is an exquisite octagonal chapel
with a 15-foot-high marble font and a poly-
chrome sculpted frieze commemorating New
York's Dutch heritage. *Amsterdam Ave. and
112th St., tel. 212/316–7540, box office tel. 212/
662–2133. Suggested donation: $2. Tours Mon.–
Sat. 11, Sun. 12:45. Open daily 7–5.*

7 At 116th Street and Amsterdam, you can pass
through the campus gates of **Columbia University,** a wealthy, private, coed institution that is
New York City's only Ivy League school. The
gilded crowns on the black wrought-iron gates
serve as a reminder that this was originally
King's College when it was founded in 1754, before American independence. Walk along the
herringbone patterned brick paths of College
Walk into the refreshingly green main quadrangle, dominated by massive neoclassical **Butler
Library** to your left (south) and the rotunda-

topped **Low Memorial Library** to your right
(north). Butler, built in 1934, holds the bulk of
the university's 4½ million books; Low, built in
1895–97 by McKim, Mead & White (who laid out
the general campus plan when the college moved
here in 1897), is now mostly offices, but on weekdays you can go inside to see its domed, temple-
like former Reading Room. The steps of Low
Library, presided over by Daniel Chester
French's statue Alma Mater, have been a focal
point for campus life, not least during the stu-
dent riots of 1968. Here Dan Aykroyd and Bill
Murray, playing recently fired Columbia research scientists, hit upon the idea of going into
business as Ghostbusters.

❽ Across Broadway from Columbia is its sister institution, **Barnard College,** established in 1889.
One of the former Seven Sisters of women's col-
leges, Barnard has steadfastly remained a sin-
gle-sex institution and has maintained its
independence from Columbia, although its students can take classes there (and vice versa).
Note the bear (the college's mascot) on the
shield above the main gates at 117th Street.
Through the gates is **Barnard Hall,** its brick-
and-limestone design echoing Columbia's buildings. Turn right to follow the path north
through the narrow but neatly landscaped campus; turn left from the main gate to peek into a
quiet residential quadrangle.

❾ Across Riverside Drive, in Riverside Park,
stands the General Grant National Memorial
Monument, commonly known as **Grant's Tomb,**
where Civil War general and two-term president Ulysses S. Grant rests beside his wife, Julia Dent Grant. The white granite mausoleum,
with its imposing columns and classical pediment, is modeled after Les Invalides in Paris,
where Napoleon is buried. Under a small white
dome, the Grants' twin black marble sarcophagi
are sunk into a deep circular chamber, which
you view from above; minigalleries to the sides
display photographs and Grant memorabilia. In
contrast to this austere monument, the surrounding plaza features wacky 1960s-era mosaic
benches, designed by local schoolchildren. *Riverside Dr. and 122nd St., tel. 212/666–1640. Admission free. Open Wed.–Sun. 9–4:30.*

Just south of Grant's Tomb, on Riverside Drive
10 at 120th Street, **Riverside Church** is a modern
(1930) Gothic-style edifice whose smooth, pale
limestone walls seem the antithesis of St. John
the Divine's rough gray hulk; in fact, it feels
more akin to Rockefeller Center, not least because John D. Rockefeller was a major benefac-
tor of the church. While most of the building
is refined and restrained, the main entrance,
on Riverside Drive, explodes with elaborate
stone carving (modeled after the French cathedral of Chartres, as are many other decorative
details here). Inside, look at the handsomely
ornamented main sanctuary, which seats only
half as many people as St. John the Divine does;
if elevator renovations have been completed,
take the elevator to the top of the 22-story, 356-
foot tower (admission: $1), with its 74-bell caril-
lon, the largest in the world. Although affiliated
with the Baptist church and the United Church
of Christ, Riverside is basically nondenomina-
tional, interracial, international, extremely political, and socially conscious. Its calendar
includes political and community events, dance
and theater programs, and concerts, along with
regular Sunday services at 10:45 AM. *Tel. 212/
222–5900. Open daily 9–5; Sun. service 10:45.*

Tour 6: Greenwich Village

*Numbers in the margin correspond to points of
interest on the Greenwich Village map.*

Greenwich Village, which New Yorkers almost
invariably speak of simply as "the Village," enjoyed a raffish reputation for years. Originally a
rural outpost of the city—a haven for New Yorkers during early 19th-century smallpox and yellow fever epidemics—many of its blocks still
look somewhat pastoral, with brick town houses
and low-rises, tiny green parks and hidden
courtyards, and a crazy-quilt pattern of narrow,
tree-lined streets.

Several generations of writers and artists have
lived and worked here: in the 19th century, Henry James, Edgar Allan Poe, Mark Twain, Walt
Whitman, and Stephen Crane; at the turn of the
century, O. Henry, Edith Wharton, Theodore
Dreiser, and Hart Crane; and during the 1920s

and '30s, John Dos Passos, Norman Rockwell, Sinclair Lewis, John Reed, Eugene O'Neill, Edward Hopper, and Edna St. Vincent Millay. In the late 1940s and early 1950s, the Abstract Expressionist painters Franz Kline, Jackson Pollock, Mark Rothko, and Willem de Kooning congregated here, as did the Beat writers Jack Kerouac, Allen Ginsberg, and Lawrence Ferlinghetti. The 1960s brought folk musicians and poets, notably Bob Dylan and Peter, Paul, and Mary.

❶ Begin a tour of Greenwich Village at Washington Arch in **Washington Square** at the foot of Fifth Avenue. Designed by Stanford White, a wood version of Washington Arch was built in 1889 to commemorate the 100th anniversary of George Washington's presidential inauguration and was originally placed about half a block north of its present location. The arch was reproduced in stone in 1892, and the statues— *Washington at War* on the left, *Washington at Peace* on the right—were added in 1913. Body builder Charles Atlas modeled for *Peace*.

Washington Square started out as a cemetery, principally for yellow fever victims, and an estimated 10,000–22,000 bodies lie below. In the early 1800s it was a parade ground and the site of public executions; bodies dangled from a conspicuous Hanging Elm that still stands at the northwest corner of the square. Later Washington Square became the focus of a fashionable residential neighborhood and a center of outdoor activity.

Most of the buildings bordering Washington Square belong to New York University. **The Row,** a series of Federal-style town houses along Washington Square North between Fifth Avenue and University Place, now serves as faculty housing. At 7–13 Washington Square North, in fact, only the fronts were preserved, with a large Fifth Avenue apartment building taking over the space behind. Developers were not so tactful when they demolished 18 Washington Square, once the home of Henry James's grandmother, which he later used as the setting for his novel *Washington Square* (Henry himself was born just off the square, in a long-gone

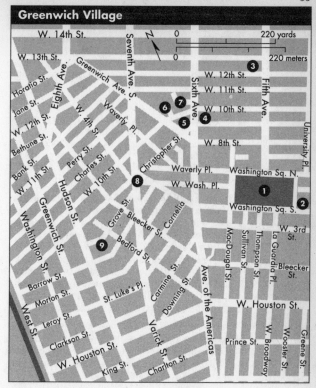

Greenwich Village

Balducci's, **4**

Forbes Magazine
Galleries, **3**

Grey Art
Gallery, **2**

Grove Court, **9**

Jefferson Market
Library, **5**

Milligan Place, **7**

Patchin Place, **6**

Sheridan
Square, **8**

Washington
Square, **1**

house on Washington Place). The house at 20 Washington Square North is the oldest building (1820) on the block. Notice its Flemish bond brickwork—alternate bricks inserted with the smaller surface (headers) facing out—which before 1830 was considered the best way to build stable walls.

On the east side of the square, NYU's main building contains the **Grey Art Gallery,** whose changing exhibitions usually focus on contemporary art. *33 Washington Pl., tel. 212/998–6780. Suggested donation: $2.50. Open Sept.–May, Tues., Thurs. and Fri. 11–6:30, Wed. 11–8:30, Sat. 11–5; June–Aug., weekdays 11–7.*

Go up Fifth Avenue half a block to **Washington Mews,** a cobblestoned private street lined on one side with the former stables of the houses on The Row. Writer Walter Lippmann and artist-patron Gertrude Vanderbilt Whitney (founder of the Whitney Museum) once had homes in the mews; today it's mostly owned by NYU. A similar Village mews, **MacDougal Alley,** can be found between Eighth Street and the square just off MacDougal Street, one block west.

Walk up Fifth Avenue, past the **Church of the Ascension** (Fifth Ave. and West 10th St.), a Gothic-style brownstone designed by Richard Upjohn. Inside, you can admire stained-glass windows by John LaFarge and a marble altar sculpture by Augustus Saint-Gaudens. In 1844, President John Tyler married Julia Gardiner here. Just past 12th Street, you can stop in the **Forbes Magazine Galleries,** where the late publisher Malcolm Forbes's idiosyncratic personal collection is on display. Highlights include intricate model boats, jeweled Fabergé eggs, and some 12,000 toy soldiers. *62 Fifth Ave., at 12th St., tel. 212/206–5548. Admission free. Open Tues.–Wed. and Fri.–Sat. 10–4.*

Backtrack on Fifth Avenue to **West 11th Street** and turn right to see one of the best examples of a Village town house block. One exception to the general 19th-century redbrick look is the modern, angled front window of 18 West 11th Street, usually occupied by a stuffed bear whose outfit changes from day to day. This house was built after the original was destroyed in a 1970 explosion; the owners' radical daughter, Kathy Boudin, had started a bomb factory in the basement with her Weathermen friends. At the time, actor Dustin Hoffman lived next door at No. 16; he was seen on TV news trying to rescue his personal possessions. Hoffman's costar in *The Graduate*, Anne Bancroft, later lived down at 52 West 11th Street with her husband, director Mel Brooks. At the end of the block, behind a low gray stone wall on the south side of the street, is the **Second Shearith Israel graveyard**, used by the country's oldest Jewish congregation after the cemetery in Chinatown (*see* Tour 9, *below*).

④ On Avenue of the Americas (Sixth Avenue), turn left to sample the wares at **Balducci's** (6th Ave. and 9th St.), a full-service gourmet food store that sprouted from the vegetable stand of the late Louis Balducci, Sr. Along with more than 80 Italian cheeses and 50 kinds of bread, this family-owned enterprise features imported Italian specialties and a prodigious selection of fresh seafood.

⑤ Directly opposite, the triangle formed by West 10th Street, Sixth Avenue, and Greenwich Avenue originally held a greenmarket, a jail, and the magnificent towered courthouse that is now the **Jefferson Market Library**. Critics variously termed the courthouse's hodgepodge of styles Venetian, Victorian, or Italian; Villagers, noting the alternating wide bands of red brick and narrow strips of granite, dubbed it the Lean Bacon Style. Over the years, the structure has housed a number of government agencies (public works, civil defense, census bureau, police academy); it was on the verge of demolition when public-spirited citizens saved it and turned it into a public library in 1967. Note the fountain at the corner of West 10th Street and Sixth Avenue, and the seal of the City of New York on the east front; inside, look at the handsome interior doorways and climb the graceful circular stairway. If the gate is open, visit the flower garden behind the library, a project run by local green thumbs.

Just west of Sixth Avenue on 10th Street is the
wrought-iron gateway to a tiny courtyard called
⑥ **Patchin Place**; around the corner, on Sixth Avenue just north of 10th Street, is a similar cul-de-
⑦ sac, **Milligan Place,** which few New Yorkers
even know is there. Both were built around 1850
for the waiters (mostly Basques) who worked at
the high-society Brevoort Hotel, long ago demolished, on Fifth Avenue. Patchin Place later
became home to several writers, including Theodore Dreiser, e.e. cummings, and Djuna
Barnes.

Take Christopher Street, which veers off from
the southern end of the library triangle, a few
steps to **Gay Street.** A curved lane lined with
small row houses circa 1810, Gay Street was
originally a black neighborhood and later a strip
of speakeasies. Ruth McKinney lived and wrote
My Sister Eileen in the basement of No. 14, and
Howdy Doody was designed in the basement of
No. 12. At the end of Gay Street go west on
Waverly Place to Christopher Street.

Time Out Where Christopher meets Grove and Waverly
Place, **Pierre's** (170 Waverly Pl., tel. 212/929-
7194) is everyone's favorite little French corner
bistro. The sumptuous couscous and the
profiteroles are two specialties. Music may include guitar or piano during dinner at this relaxed, friendly place.

As you go west on Christopher Street, you'll
pass steps leading down to the **Lion's Head** (59
Christopher St.), a longtime hangout for literary types. Before she found stardom, Jessica
Lange was a waitress here. The restaurant
faces onto a green triangle that's technically
called **Christopher Park,** but it contains a statue
of Civil War general Philip Sheridan; this con-
fuses New Yorkers, because there's another triangle to the south (between Washington Place,
Barrow Street, and Seventh Avenue) called
⑧ **Sheridan Square.** Formerly covered with as-
phalt, Sheridan Square was recently landscaped following an extensive dig by urban
archaeologists, who unearthed artifacts dating
back to the Dutch and Native American eras.

Sheridan Square was the site of a nasty 1863 riot in which a group of freed slaves were nearly lynched; in 1969, gays and police clashed nearby during a protest march that galvanized the gay rights movement. Across the busy intersection of Seventh Avenue, **Christopher Street** comes into its own as the symbolic heart of New York's gay community. Many bars and stores along here cater to that clientele, although the street is by no means off-limits to other people.

West of Seventh Avenue, the Village turns into a picture-book town of twisting, tree-lined streets, quaint houses, and tiny restaurants. Follow Grove Street from Sheridan Square past the house where Thomas Paine died (59 Grove St.) and the boyhood home of poet Hart Crane (45 Grove St.).

Time Out   **The Pink Tea Cup** (42 Grove St.) is a typical Village restaurant only insofar as it is quirky and one-of-a-kind. Stop here if you have a hankering for down-home hamhocks, chitterlings, or fried pork chops; more standard fare is featured on the menu as well, but it's all incredibly cheap.

The secluded intersection of Grove and Bedford streets seems to have fallen through a time warp into the 19th century. On the northeast corner stands one of the few remaining clapboard structures in the city (17 Grove St.); wood construction was banned as a fire hazard in 1822, the year it was built. The house has since served many functions; it housed a brothel during the Civil War. Behind it, at 102 Bedford Street, is **Twin Peaks,** an 1835 house that was rather whimsically altered in the 1920s, with stucco, half-timbers, and a pair of steep roof peaks added on.

❾ Grove Street curves in front of the iron gate of **Grove Court,** an enclave of brick-fronted town houses from the mid-1800s. Built originally as apartments for employees at neighborhood hotels, Grove Court used to be called Mixed Ale Alley because of the residents' propensity to pool beverages brought from work. It now houses a more affluent crowd: A town house there recently sold for $3 million.

Return along Bleecker Street to MacDougal Street and turn left.

Time Out The neighborhood's oldest coffeehouse is **Caffe Reggio** (119 MacDougal St., tel. 212/475–9557), where an antique machine steams forth espresso and cappuccino. The tiny tables are close together, but the crowd usually makes for interesting eavesdropping.

At **Minetta Tavern** (113 MacDougal St.), a venerable Village watering hole, turn right onto **Minetta Lane,** which leads to narrow **Minetta Street,** another former speakeasy alley. Both streets follow the course of Minetta Brook, which once flowed through this neighborhood and still bubbles deep beneath the pavement.

The foot of Minetta Street returns you to the corner of Sixth Avenue and Bleecker Street, where you reach the stomping grounds of 1960s-era folksingers (many of them performed at the now-defunct Folk City one block north on West 3rd Street). This area still attracts a young crowd—partly because of the proximity of NYU—to its cafés, bars, jazz clubs, coffeehouses, theaters, and cabarets (*see* Chapter 6), not to mention its long row of unpretentious ethnic restaurants.

Tour 7: SoHo

Numbers in the margin correspond to points of interest on the SoHo, Little Italy, and Chinatown map.

Today SoHo is virtually synonymous with a certain postmodern chic—an amalgam of black-clad artists, hip young Wall Streeters, track-lit loft apartments, hot art galleries, and restaurants with a minimalist approach to both food and decor. It's all very urban, very cool, very now. But 25 years ago, it was a virtual wasteland. SoHo (so named because it is the district *So*uth of *Ho*uston Street, bounded by Broadway, Canal Street, and Sixth Avenue) was described in a 1962 City Club of New York study as "commercial slum number one." It was saved by two factors: (1) preservationists discovered here the world's greatest concentration of cast-iron architecture and fought to prevent demolition, and (2) artists discovered the large, cheap, well-lit spaces that cast-iron buildings provide. At first it was technically illegal for artists to live in their loft studios, but so many did that eventually the zoning laws were changed to permit residence.

Walk up Greene Street, where the block between Canal and Grand streets contains the longest continuous row of cast-iron buildings anywhere (Nos. 8–34 Greene St.). The architectural rage between 1860 and 1890, cast-iron buildings were popular because they did not require massive walls to bear the weight of the upper stories. With no need for load-bearing walls, they were able to have more interior space and larger windows. They were also versatile, with various architectural elements produced from standardized molds to mimic any style—Italianate, Victorian Gothic, neo-Grecian, to name but a few visible in SoHo. Look, for example, at 28–30 Greene Street, an 1873 building nicknamed the **Queen of Greene Street.** Besides its pale paint job, notice how many decorative features have been applied: dormers, columns, window arches, and projecting central bays. Handsome as they are, these buildings were always commercial, containing stores and light manufacturing, principally textiles. Along this street notice the iron loading docks and the sidewalk vault covers studded with glass disks to let light into basement storage areas. In front of 62–64 Greene Street there's one of the few remaining turn-of-the-century bishop's-crook lampposts, with various cast-iron curlicues from the base to the curved top.

At 72–76 Greene Street is the so-called **King of Greene Street,** a five-story Renaissance-style building with a magnificent projecting porch of Corinthian columns. Today the King (now painted yellow) houses three art galleries—**Ariel, Condeso/Lawler,** and **M-13**—plus **The Second Coming,** which sells vintage clothing, furniture, and other curiosities.

At the northeast corner of Prince and Greene streets, turn to look at the corner diagonally opposite for a rare glimpse of the side of an

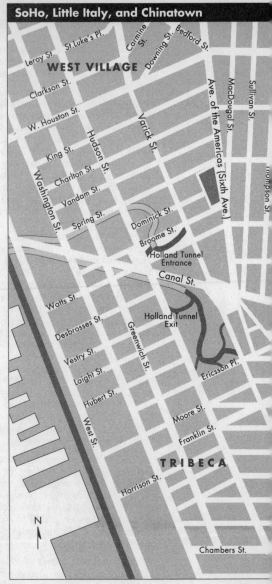

SoHo, Little Italy, and Chinatown

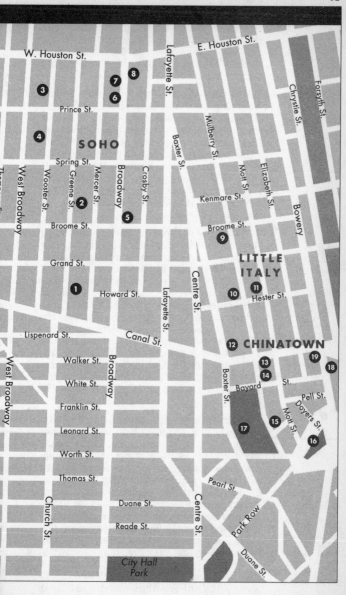

iron-front building. You'll see the same window pattern and decoration continued, with one window open and a cat sitting on the sill—where it has sat since 1973, when artist Richard Haas first painted this meticulously realistic **mural** on the blank side wall.

Take Prince Street west to Wooster Street, which, like a few other SoHo streets, still has its 19th-century pavement of Belgian blocks, a smoother successor to traditional cobblestones. At 141 Wooster Street, one of several outposts of the DIA Art Foundation, you can visit the ③ **New York Earth Room,** Walter de Maria's avantgarde 1977 artwork that consists of 140 tons of gently sculpted soil filling a second-floor gallery. *Tel. 212/473-8072. Admission free. Open Wed.-Sat. noon-6.*

At 131 Wooster Street, a store named **Home Town** has the serendipitous quality of an upscale flea market, an eclectic stock of "found objects" for making trendy lofts feel homey. Across the street is a SoHo newcomer, the **Gagosian Gallery** (136 Wooster St.), operated by prominent uptown dealer Larry Gagosian. Below Prince Street is a defiantly untrendy museum, the ④ **Museum of Colored Glass and Light,** where illuminated stained-glass pictures are mounted in a sort of dimly lit wooden maze. The artist, Russian immigrant Raphael Nemeth, runs the museum himself but isn't very talkative. *72 Wooster St., tel. 212/226-7258. Admission: $1. Open daily 1-5.*

West Broadway (which, somewhat confusingly, runs parallel to and four blocks west of regular Broadway) is SoHo's main drag, and on Saturday it can be crowded with smartly dressed uptowners and suburbanites who've come down for a little store- and gallery-hopping (*see* Chapter 3). In the block between Prince and Spring streets alone there are three major art stops: **420 West Broadway,** with six separate galleries including two of the biggest SoHo names, Leo Castelli and the Sonnabend Gallery; the **Mary Boone Gallery** (417 West Broadway); and another excellent cluster of galleries at **415 West Broadway.** One block south, at **383 West Broadway,** OK Harris has its digs. Across the street at

386 West Broadway is **D. F. Sanders,** an excellent home design store specializing in sleek postmodern objects.

Time Out The crowded, lively **Cupping Room Cafe** (359 West Broadway, tel. 212/925-2898) specializes in comforting soups, muffins, and daily specials, as well as substantial Bloody Marys.

Go east to Broome Street and Broadway where, on the northeast corner, you'll see the sadly unrestored classic of the cast-iron genre, the **⑤ Haughwout Building** (488 Broadway), nicknamed the Parthenon of Cast Iron. Built in 1857 to house Eder Haughwout's china and glassware business, the exterior was inspired by a Venetian palazzo. Inside, it contained the world's first commercial passenger elevator, a steam-powered device invented by Elisha Graves Otis.

Head north up Broadway, which temporarily loses its SoHo ambience in the midst of discount clothing stores. Just below Prince Street, the 1907 **Singer Building** (561 Broadway) shows the final flower of the cast-iron style, with wrought-iron balconies, terra-cotta panels, and broad expanses of windows. Across the street is one of New York's gourmet shrines, the gleaming **Dean & DeLuca** food market (560 Broadway), whose bread and produce arrangements often are worthy of still-life paintings. The smartly restored **560 Broadway** building also houses a respected multigallery exhibit space; another such space is just up the street at **568 Broadway.** On the ground floor at 568 Broadway is the **Armani Exchange** store, featuring a new line by the famous Italian designer—casual, basic clothes like those sold at The Gap, just right for fashion in a recession.

On the west side of Broadway, the Guggenheim Museum opened a SoHo branch in 1992: the **⑥ Guggenheim Museum SoHo,** which displays a revolving series of exhibitions, both contemporary work and pieces from the Guggenheim's permanent collection. *575 Broadway, tel. 212/ 423-3500. Admission: $5 adults, $3 senior citizens and students, children under 12 free. Open Sun., Mon., Wed. 11-6; Thurs.-Sat. 11-10.*

7 A few doors up the street, the **New Museum of Contemporary Art** shows experimental, often radically innovative work by unrecognized artists, none of it more than 10 years old. *583 Broadway, tel. 212/219–1222. Suggested donation: $3.50 adults, $2.50 students, senior citizens, and artists. Open Wed., Thurs., and Sun. noon–6; Fri. and Sat. noon–8.*

8 Across Broadway, the **Alternative Museum,** a gallery that exhibits art with a political or sociopolitical twist, has moved up to SoHo from its former TriBeCa home. *594 Broadway, tel. 212/966–4444. Suggested donation: $3. Open Tues.– Sat. 11–6.*

Tour 8: Little Italy

Numbers in the margin correspond to points of interest on the SoHo, Little Italy, and Chinatown map.

Mulberry Street is the heart of Little Italy; in fact, at this point it's virtually the entire body. In 1932 an estimated 98% of the inhabitants of this area were of Italian birth or heritage, but since then the growth and expansion of neighboring Chinatown has encroached on the Italian neighborhood to such an extent that merchants and community leaders of the Little Italy Restoration Association (LIRA) negotiated a truce in which the Chinese agreed to let at least Mulberry remain an all-Italian street.

At the southwest corner of Broome and Mulberry streets, stairs lead down through a glass entrance to what seems to be a blue-tiled cave—
9 and, appropriately enough, it is the **Grotta Azzurra** (Blue Grotto) restaurant (387 Broome St., tel. 212/925–8775), a longtime favorite for both the hearty food and the very Italian ambience. Across Mulberry Street is **Caffe Roma** (385 Broome St., 212/226–8413), a traditional pastry shop where you can eat cannoli at postage-stamp-size wrought-iron tables.

At the corner of Mulberry and Grand streets, stop to get the lay of the land. Facing north (uptown), on your right you'll see a series of wide, four-story houses from the early 19th century, built long before the great flood of immigration

hit this neighborhood between 1890 and 1924.
Turn and look south along the east side of Mulberry Street to see Little Italy's predominant
architecture today: tenement buildings with
fire escapes projecting over the sidewalks. Most
of these are of the late-19th-century New York
style known as railroad flats: six-story buildings
on 25-by-90-foot lots, with all the rooms in each
apartment placed in a straight line like railroad
cars. This style was common in the densely pop-
ulated immigrant neighborhoods of lower Manhattan until 1901, when the city passed an
ordinance requiring air shafts in the interior of
buildings. On the southeast corner, **E. Rossi &
Co.** (established in 1902) is an antiquated little
shop that sells housewares, espresso makers,
embroidered religious postcards, and jocular
Italian T-shirts. Down Grand Street is **Ferrara's**
(195 Grand St., tel. 212/226–6150), a 100-year-
old pastry shop that ships its creations—
cannoli, peasant pie, Italian rum cake—all over
the world. Another survivor of the pretenement
era is at 149 Mulberry Street, formerly the Van
Rensselaer House (built in 1816); notice its dor-
mer windows. Today it houses **Paolucci's Restaurant.**

⓾ **Umberto's Clam House** (129 Mulberry St., tel.
212/431–7545) is perhaps best known as the
place where mobster Joey Gallo was munching
scungilli in 1973 when he was fatally surprised
by a task force of mob hit men. Quite peaceful
now, Umberto's specializes in fresh shellfish in a
spicy tomato sauce. Turn onto Hester Street to
⓫ visit yet another Little Italy institution, **Puglia**
(189 Hester St., tel. 212/966–6006), a restaurant
where guests sit at long communal tables, sing
along with house entertainers, and enjoy mod-
erately priced Southern Italian specialties with
quantities of homemade wine. (For other Little
Italy restaurants, *see* Chapter 4.)

One street west, on Baxter Street toward Canal
⓬ Street, stands the **San Gennaro Church** (officially, Most Precious Blood Church, National
Shrine of San Gennaro), which each year around
September 19 sponsors Little Italy's keynote
event, the annual Feast of San Gennaro. (The
community's other big festival celebrates St.
Anthony of Padua, in June; that church is at

Houston and Sullivan streets, in what is now SoHo.) During the feasts, Little Italy's streets are closed to traffic, arches of tinsel span the thoroughfares, the sidewalks are lined with booths offering games and food, and the whole scene is one noisy, crowded, kitschy, delightful party.

Tour 9: Chinatown

Numbers in the margin correspond to points of interest on the SoHo, Little Italy, and Chinatown map.

Visibly exotic, Chinatown is a popular tourist attraction, but it is also a real, vital community, where about half of the city's population of 300,000 Chinese still live. Its main businesses are restaurants and garment factories; some 55% of its residents speak little or no English. Theoretically, Chinatown is divided from Little Italy by Canal Street, the bustling artery that links the Holland Tunnel (to New Jersey) and the Manhattan Bridge (to Brooklyn). However, in recent years, an influx of immigrants from the People's Republic of China, Taiwan, and especially Hong Kong has swelled Manhattan's Chinese population, and Hong Kong residents, anticipating the return of the British colony to PRC domination in 1997, have been investing their capital in Chinatown real estate. Consequently, Chinatown now spills over its traditional borders into Little Italy to the north and the formerly Jewish Lower East Side to the east.

Originally Canal Street was a tree-lined road with a canal running its length. Today the Chinatown stretch of Canal Street is almost overwhelmed with sidewalk markets bursting with stacks of fresh seafood and strange-shaped vegetables in extraterrestrial shades of green. Food shops proudly display their wares: If America's motto is "a chicken in every pot," then Chinatown's must be "a roast duck in every window."

❶❸ The slightly less frantic **Kam Man** (200 Canal St.), a duplex supermarket, sells an amazing assortment of fresh and canned imported groceries, herbs, and the sort of dinnerware and furniture familiar to patrons of Chinese restaurants. Choose from dozens of varieties of noodles or such delicacies as dried starch and fresh chicken feet.

14 The **Chinatown History Museum** (70 Mulberry St., 2nd floor, tel. 212/619–4785), at the corner of Bayard and Mulberry streets, shows interactive photographic exhibitions on Asian-American labor history. It also has a resource library and bookstore and offers a walking tour of Chinatown.

Mott Street, the principal business street of the neighborhood, looks the way you might expect Chinatown to look: narrow and twisting, crammed with souvenir shops and restaurants in funky pagoda-style buildings, crowded with pedestrians at all hours of the day or night. Within the few dense blocks of Chinatown, hundreds of restaurants serve every imaginable type of Chinese cuisine, from fast-food noodles or dumplings to sumptuous Hunan, Szechuan, Cantonese, Mandarin, and Shanghai feasts (*see* Chapter 4). Every New Yorker thinks he or she knows the absolute, flat-out best, but whichever one you try, at 8 PM on Saturday, don't be surprised if you have to wait in line to get in.

As you proceed down Mott Street, take a peek down Pell Street, a narrow lane of wall-to-wall restaurants whose neon signs stretch halfway across the thoroughfare.

Time Out A few steps down Pell Street, turn onto Doyers Street to find the **Viet-Nam Restaurant** (11 Doyers St., tel. 212/693–0725), an informal, inexpensive little basement restaurant that serves spicy, exotic Vietnamese dishes.

15 At the corner of Mott and Mosco streets stands the **Church of the Transfiguration.** Built in 1801 as the Zion Episcopal Church, this imposing Georgian structure with Gothic windows is now a Chinese Catholic church where mass is said in Cantonese and Mandarin.

16 At the end of Mott Street is **Chatham Square,** which is really more of a labyrinth than a square: 10 streets converge here, creating pandemonium for cars and a nightmare for pedestrians. A Chinese arch honoring Chinese casualties in American wars stands on an island in the eye of the storm. On the far end of the square, at the corner of Catherine Street and East Broadway, you'll see a branch of the Manhattan Savings Bank, built to resemble a pagoda (in this neighborhood, even some public phone booths have been styled as pagodas).

Skirting Chatham Square, head back to the right to go down Worth Street. The corner of Worth, Baxter, and Park streets was once known as Five Points, the central intersection of a tough 19th-century slum of Irish and German immigrants. Today it has been replaced by **⑰ Columbus Park,** a shady, paved urban space where children play and elderly Chinese gather to reminisce about their homelands.

Go back past Chatham Square and up the Bow- **⑱** ery to **Confucius Plaza,** the open area monitored by a statue of Confucius and the sweeping curve of a redbrick high-rise apartment complex named for him. At 18 Bowery, at the corner of Pell Street, stands one of Manhattan's oldest homes, a Federal and Georgian structure built in 1785 by meat wholesaler Edward Mooney. A **⑲** younger side of Chinatown is shown at the **Asian American Arts Center,** which displays current work by Asian American artists. *26 Bowery, tel. 212/233–2154. Admission free. Open weekdays 11–6.*

For some exotic shopping, duck into the **Canal Arcade,** a passage linking the Bowery and Elizabeth Street. A few doors down, at 50 Bowery, you'll see the **Silver Palace** restaurant (*see* Chapter 4), worth a peek inside for its Chinese rococo interior, complete with dragons whose eyes are blinking lights.

Tour 10: Lower Manhattan

Numbers in the margin correspond to points of interest on the Lower Manhattan map.

Lower Manhattan doesn't cover many acres but it is packed with attractions, for it has always been central to the city's networks of power and wealth. It was here that the New Amsterdam colony was established by the Dutch in 1625; in 1789, the first capital building of the United

States was located here. The city did not really expand beyond these precincts until the middle of the 19th century. Today lower Manhattan is in many ways dominated by Wall Street, which is both an actual street and a shorthand name for the vast, powerful financial community that clusters around the New York and American stock exchanges.

Because there's so much to see down here, you may want to break up this tour over a couple of days, depending on which attractions you choose to visit at length.

Our tour begins at the southernmost point of Manhattan, at the **Staten Island Ferry Terminal** (for subway riders, that's just outside the South Ferry station on the No. 1 line). The **Staten Island Ferry** is still the best deal in town: The 20- to 30-minute ride across New York Harbor provides great views of the Manhattan skyline, the Statue of Liberty, the Verrazano Narrows Bridge, and the New Jersey coast—and it costs only 50¢. A word of advice, however: While commuters love the ferry service's swift new low-slung craft, the boats ride low in the water and have no outside deck space. Wait for one of the higher, more open old-timers.

To the west of South Ferry lies **Battery Park,** a verdant landfill, loaded with monuments and sculpture, at Manhattan's green toe. The park's name refers to a line of cannons once mounted here to defend the shoreline (which ran along what is currently State Street). Head north along the water's edge to the **East Coast Memorial,** a statue of a fierce eagle that presides over eight granite slabs inscribed with the names of U.S. servicemen who died in the Western Atlantic during World War II. Climb the steps of the East Coast Memorial for a fine view of the main features of **New York Harbor;** from left to right: **Governors Island,** a Coast Guard installation; hilly **Staten Island** in the distance; the **Statue of Liberty** on Liberty Island; **Ellis Island,** gateway to the New World for generations of immigrants; and the old railway terminal in **Liberty State Park,** on the mainland in Jersey City, New Jersey.

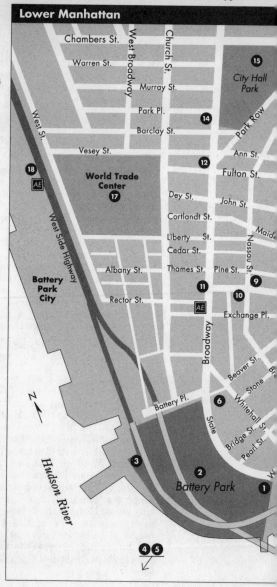

Alexander
Hamilton
Customs
House, 6
Battery Park, 2
Brooklyn
Bridge, 16
Castle Clinton, 3
City Hall, 15
Ellis Island, 5
Federal Hall
National
Memorial, 9
Fraunces
Tavern, 8
New York Stock
Exchange, 10
St. Paul's
Chapel, 12
South Street
Seaport, 13
Staten Island
Ferry
Terminal, 1
Statue of
Liberty, 4
Trinity
Church, 11
Vietnam
Veterans
Memorial, 7
Woolworth
Building, 14
World Financial
Center, 18
World Trade
Center, 17

Lower Manhattan

Chambers St.
Warren St.
West Broadway
Church St.
Murray St.
Park Pl.
Barclay St.
Vesey St.
West St.
World Trade Center
Dey St.
Cortlandt St.
Liberty St.
Cedar St.
Albany St.
Thames St.
Rector St.
West Side Highway
Battery Park City
Battery Pl.
Hudson River
City Hall Park
Park Row
Ann St.
Fulton St.
John St.
Maiden
Nassau St.
Pine St.
Exchange Pl.
Broadway
Beaver St.
Stone
Whitehall St.
Bridge St.
Pearl St.
State
Battery Park

N

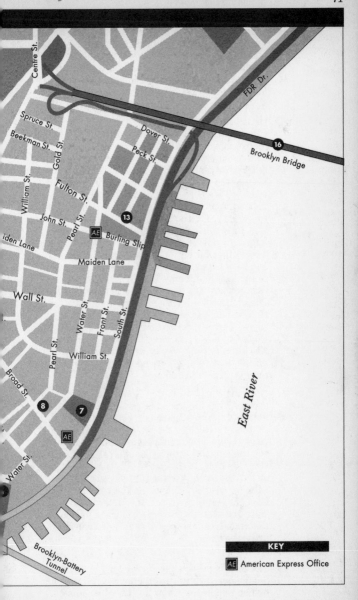

Centre St.

Spruce St.

Beekman St.

Gold St.

Dover St.

Peck St.

FDR Dr.

Brooklyn Bridge

16

William St.

Fulton St.

John St.

Pearl St.

AE Burling Slip

13

iden Lane

Maiden Lane

Wall St.

Water St.

Front St.

South St.

East River

Pearl St.

William St.

Broad St.

8

7

AE

Water St.

Brooklyn-Battery
Tunnel

KEY

AE American Express Office

Continue north past a romantic **statue of Giovanni da Verrazano,** the Florentine merchant who piloted the ship that first sighted New York and its harbor in 1524. The Verrazano Narrows Bridge between Brooklyn and Staten Island— the world's longest suspension bridge—is visible from here, just beyond Governors Island.

❸ Built in 1811 as a defense for New York Harbor, the circular brick fortress now called **Castle Clinton** was, when first built, on an island 200 feet from shore. In 1824 it became Castle Garden, an entertainment and concert facility that reached its zenith in 1850 when more than 6,000 people (the capacity of Radio City Music Hall) attended the U.S. debut of the "Swedish Nightingale," Jenny Lind. After landfill connected it to the city, Castle Clinton became, in succession, an immigrant processing center, an aquarium, and now a restored fort, museum, and ticket office for ferries to the **Statue of Liberty** and **Ellis Island.** The ferry ride is one loop; you can get off at Liberty Island, visit the statue, then reboard any ferry and continue on to Ellis Island, boarding another boat once you have finished exploring the historic immigration facility there. *Ferry information: tel. 212/269–5755. Round-trip fare: $6 adults, $5 senior citizens, $3 children 3–17. Daily departures every 45 min 9:30–3:30; more frequent departures and extended hours in summer.*

❹ After arriving on Liberty Island, you have two choices from the ground-floor entrance to the **Statue of Liberty** monument: you can take an elevator 10 stories to the top of the 89-foot-high pedestal or, if you're strong of heart and limb, you can climb 365 steps (the equivalent of a 22-story building) to the crown. (Visitors cannot go up into the torch.) Erected in 1886, the Statue of Liberty weighs 225 tons and stands 151 feet from her feet to her torch. Exhibits inside illustrate the statue's history, including videos of the view from the crown for those who don't make the climb. *Tel. 212/363–3200. Admission free.*

❺ The ferry's other stop, **Ellis Island,** opened in September 1990 to record crowds after a $140 million restoration. Now a national monument,

Ellis Island was once a federal immigration facility that processed 17 million men, women, and children between 1892 and 1954—the ancestors of more than 40% of Americans living today. The island's main building contains the **Ellis Island Immigration Museum,** with exhibits detailing not only the island's history but the whole history of immigration to America. Perhaps the most moving exhibit is the American Immigrant Wall of Honor, where the names of nearly 200,000 immigrant Americans are inscribed along an outdoor promenade overlooking the Statue of Liberty and the Manhattan skyline. *Tel. 212/363-3200. Admission free.*

A broad mall that begins at the landward entrance to Castle Clinton leads back across the park to the **Netherlands Memorial,** a quaint flagpole depicting the bead exchange that bought from the Native Americans the land to establish Fort Amsterdam in 1626. Inscriptions describe the event in English and Dutch.

❻ As you leave the park, across State Street you'll see the imposing **Alexander Hamilton Customs House,** built in 1907 in the ornate Beaux Arts style fashionable at the time. Above the base, the facade features massive columns rising to a pediment topped by a double row of statuary. Daniel Chester French, better known for the statue of Lincoln in the Lincoln Memorial in Washington, DC, sculpted the lower statues, which symbolize various continents (left to right: Asia, the Americas, Europe, Africa); the upper row represents the major trading cities of the world. The Customs House facade appeared in the movie *Ghostbusters II* as the fictional New York Museum of Art. Federal bankruptcy courts are currently housed in the Customs House, and a center of the Smithsonian Institution's Museum of the American Indian is expected to open in early 1994 on the lower floors.

The Customs House faces onto **Bowling Green,** an oval greensward at the foot of Broadway that became New York's first public park in 1733. On July 9, 1776, a few hours after citizens learned about the signing of the Declaration of Independence, rioters toppled a statue of British King George III that had occupied the spot for 11

years; much of the statue's lead was melted
down into bullets. In 1783, when the occupying
British forces fled the city, they defiantly
hoisted a Union Jack on a greased, uncleated
flagpole so it couldn't be lowered; patriot John
Van Arsdale drove his own cleats into the pole to
replace the flag with the Stars and Stripes.

From Bowling Green, head south on State
Street. A stunning semicircular office tower in
reflective glass hugs the bend of the street at 17
State Street. Next door is the **Shrine of St. Elizabeth Ann Seton** (7-8 State St.). What is now the
rectory of the shrine is a redbrick Federal-style
town house with a distinctive wood portico
shaped to fit the curving street. This house was
built in 1793 as the home of the wealthy Watson
family; Mother Seton and her family lived here
from 1801 to 1803. She joined the Catholic
Church in 1805, after the death of her husband,
and went on to found the Sisters of Charity, the
first American order of nuns. In 1975 she became the first American-born saint. Masses are
held here daily.

Continue around onto Water Street, passing on
your right **New York Plaza,** a complex of high-
tech office towers linked by an underground
7 concourse. Just beyond it is the **Vietnam Veterans Memorial,** where letters from servicemen
and -women have been etched into a wall of
greenish glass.

Return to Broad Street and go one block inland
8 to **Fraunces Tavern,** a complex of five largely
19th-century buildings housing a museum, restaurant, and bar. The main building is a Colonial
home (brick exterior, cream-colored portico and
balcony) built in 1719 and converted to a tavern
in 1762. This was the site where, in 1783, George
Washington delivered a farewell address to his
officers celebrating the British evacuation of
New York; later, the building housed some offices of the fledgling U.S. government. Today
Fraunces Tavern contains two fully furnished
period rooms and other displays of 18th- and
19th-century American history. *Broad and
Pearl Sts., tel. 212/425-1778. Admission: $2.50
adults, $1 students, senior citizens, and chil-
dren under 12. Museum open weekdays 10–4.*

Time Out The brick plaza behind 85 Broad Street is flanked by a variety of small restaurants. Order a take-out meal or snack and eat it out here on the benches, where you can watch busy office workers milling past.

Head up Pearl Street to **Hanover Square,** a quiet tree-lined plaza that stood on the waterfront when the East River reached Pearl Street. This was the city's original printing house square; on the site of 81 Pearl Street, William Bradford established the first printing press in the colonies. The pirate Captain Kidd lived in the neighborhood, and the brownstone **India House** (1837) used to house the New York Cotton Exchange. Today it holds Harry's of Hanover Square, a vintage Wall Street bar.

Walk inland up Hanover Square to the rounded corner of South William and Beaver streets, where a graceful columned porch marks the entrance to **Delmonico's** restaurant, opened in 1888 on the site of an earlier Delmonico's founded in 1827. A pioneer in serving Continental cuisine, it was *the* place to go at the turn of the century; under different ownership, it is still a restaurant today.

Two blocks farther north, William Street crosses **Wall Street,** so called because it traces the course of a wood wall built across the island in 1653 to defend the Dutch colony against the native Indians. Arguably the most famous thoroughfare in the world, though only a third of a mile long, Wall Street began its financial career with stock traders conducting business along the sidewalks or at tables beneath a sheltering buttonwood tree. Today it's a dizzyingly narrow canyon—look to the right and you'll glimpse a sliver of East River waterfront; look to the left and you'll see the spire of Trinity Church, tightly framed by skyscrapers at the head of the street.

To learn the difference between Ionic and Corinthian columns, look at the **Citibank Building** to your right (55 Wall St.). The lower stories were part of an earlier U.S. Customs House, built in 1863, and it was literally a bullish day on Wall Street when oxen hauled its 16 granite Ionic columns up to the site. When the National City Bank took over the building in 1907, the architects McKim, Mead & White added a second tier of columns, but made them Corinthian.

One block west on Wall Street, where Broad Street becomes Nassau Street, you'll find on your right a regal statue of George Washington on the steps of the **Federal Hall National Memorial.** This 1883 statue by John Quincy Adams Ward marks the spot where Washington was sworn in as the first U.S. president in 1789. After the capital moved to Philadelphia in 1790, the original Federal Hall became New York's City Hall, then was demolished in 1812 when the present City Hall (*see below*) was completed. The clean and simple lines of the current structure, built as (yet another) U.S. Customs House in 1842, were modeled after the Parthenon, a potent symbol for a young nation striving to emulate classical Greek democracy. It's now a museum featuring exhibits on New York and Wall Street. *26 Wall St., tel. 212/264-8711. Admission free. Open weekdays 9-5.*

In building a two-story investment bank at the corner of Wall and Broad streets, J. P. Morgan was in effect declaring himself above the pressures of Wall Street real-estate values. Now **Morgan Guaranty Trust,** the building bears pockmarks near the fourth window on the Wall Street side, created when a bomb in a pushcart exploded in 1920.

Perhaps the heart of Wall Street is the **New York Stock Exchange,** which has its august Corinthian main entrance around the corner at 20 Broad Street. Compared with the Federal Hall memorial, this neoclassical building is much more elaborately decorated, as befitted the more grandiose national image of 1901, when it was designed. Inside, after what may be a lengthy wait, you can take an elevator to the third-floor visitor center. A self-guided tour, informative slide shows, video displays, and guides may help you interpret the seeming chaos you'll see from the visitors' gallery overlooking the immense (50-foot-high) trading hall. *Tickets available at 20 Broad St., tel. 212/656-5168. Free tickets are distributed beginning at 9:05; come*

*before noon to assure getting in. Open weekdays
9:15–3:15.*

⑪ **Trinity Church** (Broadway and Wall St.) was established as an Anglican parish in 1697. The
present structure (1846), by Richard Upjohn,
ranked as the city's tallest building for most of
the second half of the 19th century. Its three
huge bronze doors were designed by Richard
Morris Hunt to recall Ghiberti's doors for the
Baptistry in Florence, Italy. After the exterior
sandstone was restored in 1991, New Yorkers
were amazed to discover that a church they had
always thought of as black was actually a rosy
pink. The church's Gothic Revival interior is
surprisingly light and elegant, although you
may see derelicts napping in the pews. On the
church's south side is a 2½-acre graveyard: Alexander Hamilton is buried beneath a white
stone pyramid; and a monument commemorates
Robert Fulton, the inventor of the steamboat
(he's actually buried in the Livingstone family
vault, with his wife).

⑫ Head north on Broadway to **St. Paul's Chapel**
(Broadway and Fulton St.), the oldest (1766)
surviving church in Manhattan and the site of
the prayer service following George Washington's inauguration as president. Built of rough
Manhattan stone, it was modeled after London's
St. Martin-in-the-Fields. It's open until 4 (Sundays until 3) for prayer and meditation; look in
the north aisle for Washington's pew.

Walk down Fulton Street, named after the ferry
to Brooklyn that once docked at its foot (the
ferry itself was named after its inventor, Robert
Fulton), to Water Street, which was once the
shoreline. On the 19th-century landfill across
⑬ the street is the 11-block **South Street Seaport
Historic District,** which was created in 1967
to save this area from being overtaken by
skyscrapers. The Rouse Corporation, which
had already created slick so-called "festival
marketplaces" in Boston (Quincy Market) and
Baltimore (Harborplace), was later hired to re-
store and adapt the existing historic buildings.

The little white lighthouse at Water and Fulton
streets is the **Titanic Memorial,** commemorating
the sinking of the RMS *Titanic* in 1912. Beyond

it, Fulton Street, cobbled in blocks of Belgian granite, is a pedestrian mall that swarms with visitors, especially on fine-weather weekends. Immediately to your left is the **Cannon's Walk Block,** which contains 15 restored buildings.

At 211 Water Street is **Bowne & Co.,** a reconstructed working 19th-century print shop. Around the corner, a narrow court called Cannon's Walk, lined with shops, opens onto Fulton Street; follow it around to Front Street. Directly across Front Street is the **Fulton Market Building,** a modern building, full of shops and restaurants, that re-creates the bustling commercial atmosphere of the old victual markets that were on this site from 1822 on. On the south side of Fulton Street is the seaport's architectural centerpiece, **Schermerhorn Row,** a redbrick terrace of Georgian- and Federal-style warehouses and countinghouses built in 1811–12. Today the ground floors are occupied by upscale shops, bars, and restaurants, and the **South Street Seaport Museum.** *Tel. 212/669–9400. Admission to ships, galleries, walking tours, Maritime Crafts Center, films, and other seaport events: $6 adults, $5 senior citizens, $4 students, $3 children. Open fall–spring, daily 10–5; summer, daily 10–6.*

Cross South Street under an elevated stretch of the FDR Drive to **Pier 16,** where the historic ships are docked, including the *Peking,* the second-largest sailing ship in existence; the full-rigged *Wavertree;* and the lightship *Ambrose.* A restored **Pilothouse** is the pierside information center. Pier 16 is also the departure point for the 90-minute **Seaport Line Harbor Cruise.** *Tel. 212/669–9400. Fare: $12 adults, $11 senior citizens, $10 students, $6 children. Combination fares—for the cruise and the other attractions—run $15.25, $13.50, $12, and $7.50.*

To the north is **Pier 17,** a multilevel dockside shopping mall. Its weathered-wood rear decks make a splendid spot from which to sit and contemplate the river; look north to see the Brooklyn, Manhattan, and Williamsburg bridges, and look across to see Brooklyn Heights.

Time Out If you're hungry, head for the fast-food stalls on Pier 17's third-floor **Promenade Food Court.** The cuisine is nonchain eclectic: Seaport Fries, Pizza on the Pier, Wok & Roll, the Yorkville Packing House, the Salad Bowl, or Bergen's Beer & Wine Garden (10 brews on tap). What's really spectacular is the view from the tables in a glass-walled atrium.

Return along Fulton Street to Broadway and walk two blocks north to the so-called "Cathedral of Commerce," the ornate white terra-cotta **⑭** **Woolworth Building** (Park Pl. and Broadway). When it opened in 1913 it was, at 792 feet, the world's tallest building; it still houses the Woolworth corporate offices. Among its extravagant Gothic-style details are sculptures set into arches in the lobby ceiling; one of them represents old man Woolworth pinching his pennies, while another depicts the architect, Cass Gilbert, cradling in his arms a model of his creation.

Across Broadway is triangular **City Hall Park,** originally the town common. A bronze statue of patriot Nathan Hale, who was hanged as a spy by the British troops occupying New York City, stands on the Broadway side of the park. In its day this green spot has hosted hangings, riots, and demonstrations; it is also the finish line for ticker-tape parades up lower Broadway (though ticker-tape is nowadays replaced with perforated margin strips torn off from tractor-feed computer paper).

⑮ **City Hall,** built between 1803 and 1812, is unexpectedly sedate, small-scale, and charming. Its exterior columns reflect the classical influence of Greece and Rome, and the handsome cast-iron cupola is crowned with a statue of Lady Justice. Originally its front and sides were clad in white marble while the back was faced in cheap brownstone, because the city fathers assumed New York would never grow farther north than this! (Limestone now covers all four sides.) The major interior feature is a domed rotunda from which a sweeping marble double staircase leads to the second-floor public rooms. The wood-paneled City Council Chamber in the east wing is small and clubby; the Board of Estimate chamber to the west has colonial paintings and church-pew-style seating; and the Governor's Room at the head of the stairs, used for ceremonial events, is filled with historic portraits and furniture. The mayor's office is on the ground floor.

Just east of City Hall, a ramp curves up into the **16** pedestrian walkway over the **Brooklyn Bridge.** The Great Bridge promenade takes a half-hour to walk and is a New York experience on a par with the Statue of Liberty trip or the Empire State Building ascent. Before this bridge was built, Brooklynites had to rely on the Fulton Street ferry to Brooklyn—a charming way to travel, surely, but unreliable in the fog and ice of winter. After some 50 years of talk about a bridge, John Augustus Roebling, a respected engineer, was handed a bridge construction assignment in 1867. As the project to build the first steel suspension bridge slowly took shape over the next 15 years, it captured the imagination of the city; on its completion in 1883, it was called the Eighth Wonder of the World. Its twin Gothic-arched towers rise 268 feet from the river below. The roadway is supported by a web of steel cables, hung from the towers and attached to block-long anchorages on either shore. It is hardly the longest suspension bridge in the world anymore, but it remains a symbol of what man can accomplish. As you look south from the walkway, the pinnacles of downtown Manhattan loom on your right, Brooklyn Heights stands sentinel on your left, and before you yawns the harbor, with Lady Liberty showing herself in profile. Turn about for a fine view up the East River, spanned within sight by the Manhattan and Williamsburg bridges. You don't need binoculars to enjoy the vistas, but you'd do well to bring a hat or scarf, because the wind whips through the cables like a dervish.

Backtrack across Broadway and turn down **17** Church Street to the **World Trade Center,** a 16-acre, 12 million-square-foot complex that contains New York's two tallest buildings (1,350 feet high). To reach the observation deck on the 107th floor of 2 World Trade Center, elevators glide a quarter of a mile into the sky—in only 58 seconds. The view potentially extends 55 miles, although signs at the ticket window disclose how far you can see that day and whether the outdoor deck is open. *Tel. 212/435–7397. Admission: $4 adults, $2.25 senior citizens, $2 children, children under 6 free. Open daily 9:30 AM–11:30 PM.*

You can get the same view with a meal at **Windows on the World** (*see* Chapter 4) atop 1 World Trade Center; lighter meals or drinks are available at its **Hors d'Oeuvrerie** (jacket required).

Some 50,000 people work in this seven-building complex, and at street level and underground it contains more than 60 stores, services, and restaurants, as well as the adjacent New York Vista hotel. There's a TKTS booth selling discount tickets to Broadway and Off-Broadway shows (*see* Chapter 6) in the mezzanine of 2 World Trade Center (open weekdays 11–5:30, Sat. 11–1), and on the ninth floor of 4 World Trade Center, a visitors' gallery overlooks the trading floor of the Commodities Exchange (tel. 212/938–2025; open weekdays 9:30–3).

More than a million cubic yards of rock and soil were excavated for the World Trade Center—and then moved across West Street to help beget the 100-acre Battery Park City development, a complete neighborhood built from scratch. Take the pedestrian overpass north of 1 World Trade Center to Battery Park City's centerpiece, the **⓲** **World Financial Center,** a four-tower complex designed by Cesar Pelli, with some heavy-duty corporate tenants including Merrill Lynch, American Express, and Dow Jones. You'll come out into the soaring **Winter Garden Atrium,** its mauve marble cascade of steps spilling down into a vaulted plaza with 16 giant palm trees, framed by a vast arched window overlooking the Hudson. This stunning space has become a popular venue for free performances by top-flight musicians and dancers (tel. 212/945–0505). Surrounding the atrium are several upscale shops—Godiva chocolatiers, Rizzoli bookshop, Ann Taylor for women's clothing, Mark Cross for leather goods—plus a skylit food court.

Time Out While the courtyard also offers several full-
service restaurants, for a quick bite head for
Minters (tel. 212/945–4455)—and be sure to
leave room for their ice-cream cones.

Of the few spots in Manhattan that directly
overlook the rivers, **Battery Park City** just may
be the best. The outdoor plaza right behind the
atrium curls around a tidy little yacht basin;
take in the view of the Statue of Liberty and
read the stirring quotations worked into the
iron railings. Just north of the basin is the terminal for ferry service to Hoboken, New Jersey
(tel. 908/463–3779; fare: $2), on the other side of
the Hudson River. It's an eight-minute ride to
Frank Sinatra's hometown, with a spectacular
view of lower Manhattan.

To the south, a longer riverside promenade that
eventually will extend to Battery Park accompa-
nies the residential part of Battery Park City, a
mix of high rises, town houses, shops, and green
squares that does a surprisingly good job of
duplicating the rhythms of the rest of the city.
Especially noteworthy among the art works
populating the esplanade are Ned Smyth's columned plaza with chessboards; and the South
Cove, a collaborative effort, a romantic curved
stage set of wood piers and a steel-frame look-
out. Slated to open in early 1994 behind South
Cove is the **Living Memorial to the Holocaust–
Museum of Jewish Heritage** (Battery Pl. between 1st and 2nd Pl., tel. 212/687–9141).

Other Attractions

The **Bronx Zoo,** the nation's largest urban zoo
deserves nearly an entire day's visit on its own.
You can take the Liberty Lines BxM11 bus that
runs up Madison Avenue ($3.50). At the Bronx
Zoo you'll see two different historical methods
of wild-animal keeping. The turn-of-the-century zoological garden houses monkeys, sea lions,
and elephants (among many others) in fancy
Beaux Arts–style edifices at **Astor Court.** It's
being gradually replaced by the animal-in-habi-
tat approach used in the **World of Birds,** with its
capacious walk-through indoor natural habitats;
in **Jungleworld,** an indoor tropical rain forest

complete with five waterfalls, millipedes, flowering orchids, and pythons; and in the new **Baboon Reserve.** The **Children's Zoo** ($1.50 admission; open Apr.–Oct.) features many hands-on learning activities, as well as a large petting zoo. At the **Zoo Center,** visitors will find a rare Sumatran rhino. The zoo as a whole has more than 4,000 animals representing 667 species. *Bronx Park, tel. 718/367–1010. Admission: Thurs.–Tues. $5.75 adults, $2 senior citizens and children 2–12 (Nov.–Feb. $2.75 adults, $1 children), children under 2 free; Wed., voluntary contribution. Open Mar.–Oct., weekdays 10–5, weekends and holidays 10–5:30; Nov.–Feb., daily 10–4:30.*

Carnegie Hall has been hosting musical headliners since 1891, when its first concert was conducted by no less than Tchaikovsky. Outside it's a stout, square brown building with a few Moorish-style arches added, almost as an afterthought, to the facade. Inside, however, is a simply decorated, 2,804-seat auditorium that is considered one of the finest in the world. It was extensively restored a few years ago, before its gala 1990–1991 centennial season, although critics still debate whether the main auditorium's acoustics will ever be as perfect as they were before. The lobby is bigger now, though, and a museum has been added just east of the main auditorium, displaying memorabilia from the hall's illustrious history. Hour-long guided tours of Carnegie Hall are also available. *Carnegie Hall Museum: 881 7th Ave., tel. 212/903–9629. Admission free. Open daily 11–4:30. Guided tours offered Mon., Tues., and Thurs. 11:30, 2, and 3 (performance schedule permitting); admission: $6 adults, $5 students and seniors, $3 children.*

The Cloisters, perched atop a wooded hilltop near Manhattan's northernmost tip, houses the Metropolitan Museum of Art's medieval collection in the style of a medieval monastery. Colonnaded walks connect authentic French and Spanish monastic cloisters, a French Romanesque chapel, a 12th-century chapter house, and a Romanesque apse. An entire room is devoted to a superb set of 15th- and 16th-century tapestries depicting a unicorn hunt. The view of the Hudson River and the New Jersey Palisades (an undeveloped Rockefeller family preserve) enhances the experience. The M-4 "Cloisters-Fort Tryon Park" bus provides a lengthy but scenic ride; catch it along Madison Avenue below 110th Street, or Broadway above; or take the A subway to 190th Street. *Fort Tryon Park, tel. 212/923–3700. Suggested donation: $6 adult, $3 senior citizens and students, children under 12 free. Open Tues.–Sun. 9:30–5:15. Closes at 4:45 Nov.–Feb.*

The **Empire State Building** may no longer be the world's tallest building, but it is certainly one of the world's best-loved skyscrapers. The Art Deco playground for King Kong opened in 1931 after only about a year of construction. Today more than 16,000 people work in the building, and more than 2½ million people a year visit the 86th- and 102nd-floor observatories. Pass beneath the stainless-steel canopy on 34th Street to enter the three-story-high marbled lobby, where illuminated panels depicting the Seven Wonders of the World brazenly add the Empire State as the Eighth Wonder. Go to the concourse level to buy a ticket for the observation decks (here you can also visit the **Guinness World of Records Exhibition**). The 102nd-floor spot is glassed in; the 86th floor is open to the air. *5th Ave. and 34th St., tel. 212/736–3100. Admission: $3.50 adults, $1.75 children 5–11, under 5 free. Open daily 9:30 AM–midnight.*

Gracie Mansion, the official home of the mayor of New York, is located in Carl Schurz Park, which runs along the East River north of 86th Street. Surrounded by a small lawn and flowerbeds, this Federal-style yellow frame house still feels like a country manor house, which is what it was built as in 1779 by wealthy merchant Archibald Gracie. The Gracie family entertained many notable guests at the mansion, including Louis Philippe (later king of France), President John Quincy Adams, the marquis de Lafayette, Alexander Hamilton, James Fenimore Cooper, Washington Irving, and John Jacob Astor. The city purchased Gracie Mansion in 1887, and, after a period of use as the Museum of the City of New York (now at Fifth Ave. and 103rd St.—*see* Tour 3, *above*), Mayor Fiorello H.

You've Let Your Imagination Go, Now Get Up And Follow Your Dreams.

For The Vacation You're Dreaming Of, Call American Express® Travel Agency At 1-800-YES-AMEX.*

American Express will send more than your imagination soaring. We'll fly you, sail you, drive you to any Fodor's destination and beyond. Because American Express believes the best vacations happen from Europe to the Orient, Walt Disney® World to Hawaii and everywhere in between.

For dependable service, expert advice, and value wherever your dreams take you, call on American Express. After all, the best traveling companion is a trustworthy friend.

AMERICAN EXPRESS Travel Agency

It's easy to recognize a good place when you see one.

American Express Cardmembers have been doing it for years.

The secret? Instead of just relying on what they see in the window,

they look at the door. If there's an American Express Blue Box on it, they

know they've found an establishment that cares about high standards.

Whether it's a place to eat, to sleep, to shop, or simply meet, they

know they will be warmly welcomed.

So much so, they're rarely taken in by anything else.

Always a good sign.

La Guardia made it the official mayor's residence. *Free guided tours mid-Mar.–mid-Nov., Wed. at 10, 11, 1, and 2, by reservation only. Call 212/570–4751.*

The **Pierpont Morgan Library** is built around the famous banker's own study and library, completed in 1906 by McKim, Mead & White. Around the corner, at 37th Street and Madison Avenue, is the latest addition to the library, an 1852 Italianate brownstone that was once the home of Morgan's son, J. P. Morgan, Jr. The elder Morgan's own house stood at 36th Street and Madison Avenue; it was torn down after his death and replaced with the simple neoclassical annex that today holds the library's main exhibition space. Turn right just past the entrance and go down a long cloister corridor for the library's most impressive rooms: the elder Morgan's personal study, its red-damask-lined walls hung with first-rate paintings, and his majestic personal library with its dizzying tiers of handsomely bound rare books, letters, and illuminated manuscripts. *29 E. 36th St., tel. 212/685–0008. Suggested donation: $5 adults, $3 students and senior citizens. Open Tues.–Sat. 10:30–5, Sun. 1–5.*

What to See and Do with Children

New York is as magical a place for children as it is for adults. In fact, there are very few sights or activities in the city that can't be enjoyed from a pint-size perspective. Look for calendars of children's events in *New York* magazine and the *Village Voice* weekly newspaper, available at newsstands. The Friday *New York Times* also has a good listing of children's activities.

Sightseeing While you're sightseeing with your family, don't miss the **Statue of Liberty** (*see* Tour 10, *above*) or the **South Street Seaport** (*see* Tour 10, *above*), both reliable hits with children. Boat rides are also a good way to see the city with youngsters—try the **Circle Line** (Pier 83, west end of 42nd St., tel. 212/563–3200), or, for a shorter, cheaper thrill, the 50¢ ride on the **Staten Island Ferry** (terminal in Battery Park). Another fun, quick way to see the city is to ride the **Roosevelt Island Aerial Tramway** across the East River.

Trams board at Second Avenue and 60th Street; the fare is $1.40 in each direction.

Museums While just about every major museum in New York has something to interest children, certain ones hold special appeal. At the top of the list is the **American Museum of Natural History** (Central Park West at 79th St., tel. 212/769–5100), with its lifelike dioramas and giant dinosaurs (some rooms are off-limits until 1995, when the restoration of the entire collection will be completed). Especially intriguing are the Discovery Room, which features hands-on exhibits for children, and the Naturemax Theater, which shows amazing nature films on its gigantic screen. The **Hayden Planetarium** (attached to the museum) offers sky shows tailored to seasonal and special events; there is also a preschool show, for which you must make reservations (tel. 212/769–5920). (*See* Tour 5, *above*.)

The **Children's Museum of Manhattan,** designed for children ages 2–12, offers interactive exhibits organized around common childhood experiences. Children can paint, make collages, try on costumes, pet animals, and generally stay amused for hours on end. *212 W. 83rd St., tel. 212/721–1234. Admission: $4, children under 2 free. Open Mon. and Wed.–Fri. 1–5, weekends 10–5.*

Another favorite of the younger generation is the *Intrepid* **Sea-Air-Space Museum.** This famous World War II aircraft carrier brings to life the history of naval aviation, the modern U.S. Navy, and attempts at space travel. On display are more than 40 aircraft, rockets, and space vehicles, as well as an impressive collection of Congressional Medals of Honor. *Pier 86 at W. 46th St., tel. 212/245–0072. Admission: $7 adults, $6 senior citizens, $4 children ages 6–12. Open Wed.–Sun. 10–5.*

The **Forbes Magazine Galleries** (62 5th Ave., tel. 212/206–5548), with its collections of toy soldiers and toy boats, speaks to the child in all of us (*see* Tour 6, *above*). Another good bet is the **New York City Fire Museum** (278 Spring St., tel. 212/691–1303), where loads of fire-fighting equipment is on display.

Parks and Playgrounds The obvious first choice is **Central Park,** where children can ride bicycles, play tennis, row boats, go horseback riding, iceskate, rollerskate, skateboard, jog, fly kites, feed ducks, throw Frisbees—the list goes on and on. Children age 12 and under will enjoy the nostalgic **Carousel** (mid-park at 65th St., tel. 212/879–0244), complete with painted horses that prance up and down to jaunty organ music; it costs only 90¢ a ride. **Belvedere Castle** offers an inviting hands-on learning center with an emphasis on natural science. *Mid-park at 79th St., tel. 212/772–0210. Admission free. Open mid-Feb.–mid-Oct., Tues.–Thurs. and weekends 11–5, Fri. 1–5; mid-Oct.–mid-Feb., closes one hour earlier, at 4 PM.*

Central Park has several excellent adventure playgrounds, in which weathered-wood structures, often underlaid with soft sand, support slides, swings, bridges, ladders, monkey bars, and other devices that safely encourage active play. Playgrounds can be found along the park's western edge at 68th Street, 81st Street, 85th Street, 93rd Street, and 96th Street; along the eastern edge at 67th Street, 71st Street, 77th Street, 85th Street, and 95th Street; and at the large Heckscher playground mid-park at 62nd Street.

Other good public playgrounds can be found at **Battery Park City** (West St. south of Vesey St.), **Washington Square** (at the foot of 5th Ave., between Waverly Pl. and W. 4th St.), **Abingdon Square** (at the triangular junction of Hudson, Bleecker, and Bank Sts. in the West Village), **John Jay Park** (east of 1st Ave. between 76th and 78th Sts.), next to the **United Nations** Rose Garden (1st Ave. between 47th and 48th Sts.), and **Riverside Park** (west of Riverside Drive; playgrounds at 82nd and 89th Sts.).

Restaurants At South Street Seaport, Pier 17's **Promenade Food Court** offers a wide variety of quick foods to eat in a wide-open space. At the East Village's **Two Boots** (37 Ave. A, between 2nd and 3rd Sts., tel. 212/505–2276), young customers are provided with crayons and coloring books. In Chinatown, the **Silver Palace** (52 Bowery, tel. 212/964–1204) welcomes youngsters. Best

Greenwich Village bets are **Pizza Piazza** (785 Broadway at 10th St., tel. 212/505–0977), Caribbean-influenced **Bayamo** (704 Broadway at 4th St., tel. 212/475–5151), and **Elephant and Castle** (68 Greenwich Ave. at 7th Ave., tel. 212/ 243–1400. Good hamburgers are served in a casual, fun atmosphere at **Hamburger Harry's** in TriBeCa (157 Chambers St. between Hudson and Greenwich Sts., tel. 212/267–4446) and in midtown (145 W. 45th St., tel. 212/840–2756). Other midtown choices are **The Stage Delicatessen** (834 7th Ave. at 54th St., tel. 212/245/– 7850), **O'Neal Bros. Cafe** (60 W. 57th St., tel. 212/546–0300), and **Mamma Leone's** (239 W. 48th St., tel. 212/586–5151), which despite its touristy atmosphere is fun for kids. A popular East Side spot with children is **Serendipity** (225 E. 60th St., tel. 212/838–3531); if you can't get in there, try the barbecued ribs at **Tony Roma's** (400 E. 57th St., tel. 212/308–0200). On the West Side, **Presto's** (434 Amsterdam Ave. at 81st St., tel. 212/721–9141) serves up good pasta and pizza near the American Museum of Natural History; **Boulevard** (2398 Broadway at 88th St., tel. 212/874–7400) is a friendly neighborhood spot with burgers, barbecue, and a kids' menu. All of these restaurants have booster seats available, and most also have high chairs.

3 Shopping

By Karen Cure

Updated by Terry Trucco

Shopping in New York is theater, architecture, and people-watching all rolled into one. Big stores and small ones, one-of-a-kinds and chains together present an overwhelming array of "Things." There are fabulous department stores, with something for everyone, and tiny specialists.

Another important lure of Manhattan shopping is the bargain. Major intersections are instant markets as street peddlers hawk fake Gucci and Cartier watches at $15–$25 each. (These may just possibly last a year or two.) There are thrift shops and resale shops where, it's whispered, Jackie O sends her castoffs and Catherine Deneuve snaps up antique lace. At off-price and discount stores, mark-offs are, as locals say, "to die for," and the sales are even better. Designers' showroom sales allow you to buy cheap at the source; auctions promise good prices as well.

Stores are generally open Monday–Saturday from 10 AM to 5 or 6 PM, but neighborhood peculiarities do exist. In midtown and lower Manhattan, shops are often closed all weekend. Most stores on the Lower East Side close on Friday afternoon and all day Saturday for the Jewish Sabbath, while keeping normal hours on Sunday. Sunday hours, also common on the West Side and in the Village, are the exception on the Upper East Side.

Shopping Neighborhoods

South Street Seaport The Seaport's shops are located along the cobbled, pedestrians-only extension to Fulton Street; in the Fulton Market building, the original home of the city's fish market; and on the three levels of Pier 17. You'll find some of the best of the country's upscale retailers: **Ann Taylor** and **Laura Ashley** for women's clothing, **Brookstone** for fancy gadgets and hardware, **Coach** for handbags, **Caswell-Massey** for fragrances, and **Sharper Image** for high-tech gimmickry.

World Financial Center Although the nearby World Trade Center bills its concourse as the city's busiest shopping center, the World Financial Center in Battery Park City is a shopping destination to reckon with, thanks to stores such as **Barneys New York** for

A & S Plaza, **13**

575 Fifth Avenue, **9**

Barneys New York, **14**

Bergdorf Goodman, **3**

Bloomingdale's, **1**

Galeries Lafayette New York, **5**

Henri Bendel, **4**

Herald Center, **12**

Lord & Taylor, **10**

Lower East Side (Orchard Street), **15**

Macy's, **11**

Manhattan Art and Antiques Center, **6**

Place des Antiquaires, **2**

Rockefeller Center, **7**

Saks Fifth Avenue, **8**

South Street Seaport, **18**

Trump Tower, **5**

World Financial Center, **16**

World Trade Center, **17**

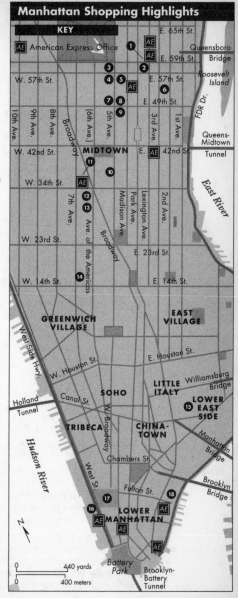

Manhattan Shopping Highlights

clothing, **Godiva Chocolatier** for chocolates, **Mark Cross** for leather goods, **Ann Taylor,** and **Caswell-Massey.** Most are open on Sundays.

Lower East Side Once home to millions of Jewish immigrants from Russia and Eastern Europe, this area is New Yorkers' bargain beat. The center of it all is narrow, unprepossessing Orchard Street, which is crammed with tiny, no-nonsense clothing and shoe stores ranging from kitschy to elegant.

SoHo On West Broadway, SoHo's main drag, and on Broadway and Wooster, Greene, Mercer, Prince, Spring, Broome, and Grand streets, major art galleries keep company with chic clothing stores such as **La Rue des Rêves** and **Victoria Falls.**

Lower Fifth Avenue Fifth Avenue south of 20th Street and the avenues fanning east and west are home to some of New York's hippest shops and a lively downtown crowd. Many of the locals sport clothes from the neighborhood—a mix of **Emporio Armani, Paul Smith,** and **Matsuda,** sometimes finished off with big black shades from **Alain Mikli. Barneys, Williams-Sonoma,** and **Pottery Barn** are also nearby, along with an enormous outpost of **Barnes & Noble.**

Herald Square Reasonable prices prevail at this intersection of 34th Street and Avenue of the Americas (Sixth Avenue). Giant **Macy's** is the linchpin. Opposite, in glittering Herald Center (the former E. J. Korvette—the original Saks & Company), the chief draw is Manhattan's first **Toys "Я" Us.** Next door on Sixth Avenue, the new **A&S Plaza** atrium-mall is anchored by the Manhattan outlet of the Brooklyn-based A&S department store, which makes for wonderful browsing.

Midtown Near Grand Central The biggest men's clothiers are here on and just off the stretch of Madison Avenue nicknamed "Trad Avenue": **J. Press; Brooks Brothers; Paul Stuart; F. R. Tripler;** and **Wallachs.** Most also handle women's clothing in dress-for-success styles.

Fifth Avenue The boulevard that was once home to some of the biggest names in New York retailing is not what it once was, that role having been usurped by Madison Avenue north of 57th Street. But

Fifth Avenue from Central Park South to Rockefeller Center still shines with **F.A.O. Schwarz** and **Bergdorf Goodman** (both the main store and **Bergdorf Goodman Men** are at 58th St.), **Tiffany** and **Bulgari** jewelers (at 57th St.), the various luxury stores in **Trump Tower** (at 56th St.), **Henri Bendel,** across the street, **Steuben** glassware and **Ferragamo** shoes (at 55th St.), **Cartier** jewelers (at 52nd St.), and so on down to **Saks Fifth Avenue** (at 50th St.). **Rockefeller Center** itself provides a plethora of shops. To the south (at 47th St.) is the shiny 575 atrium mall, named for its Fifth Avenue address.

57th Street East of Fifth you'll find the new **Galeries Lafayette New York,** a branch of the famous French department store, and such exclusive stores as **Chanel; Burberrys; Escada; Hermès;** and the **Place des Antiquaires** antiques shop complex. Above and alongside these stores are top art galleries such as **André Emmerich** and **Pace.**

Columbus Avenue Between 66th and 86th streets, this former tenement district is now home to some of the city's glitziest stores. Shops are mostly modern in design, upscale but not top-of-the-line. Clothing runs the gamut from preppy for men and women (**Frank Stella Ltd.**) to high funk (**Betsey Johnson**) and high style (**Charivari**). It's a good source for fine costume jewelry (**Ylang Ylang**). Children will enjoy stops at **Mythology** and **Penny Whistle Toys.**

Upper East Side Along Madison and Lexington avenues, roughly between 57th and 79th streets, New York branches of world-renowned designer emporiums are joined by a group of spirited retailers who fill their stores with the unique and the stylish. Items for the home, fine antiques, and wonderful clothing predominate—and the prices aren't always sky-high.

Department Stores

A&S (33rd St. and 6th Ave., tel. 212/594–8500). The old Gimbel's, a block south of Macy's, lives again as home to A&S Plaza, whose nine floors are anchored by Abraham & Straus, well established in the outer boroughs.

Bergdorf Goodman (754 5th Ave., between 57th and 58th Sts., tel. 212/753–7300). Good taste reigns in an elegant and understated setting. The Home Department is room after exquisite room of wonderful linens, tabletop items, and gifts. The expanded men's store, across the street, occupies the former home of the giant F.A.O. Schwarz toy store.

Bloomingdale's (1000 3rd Ave. at 59th St., tel. 212/355–5900). Its main floor is a stupefying maze of mirrors and black walls; elsewhere the racks are overfull, salespeople overworked, and the departments constantly on the move. Still, selections are dazzling at all but the lowest price points, and the markdowns on top-of-the-line designer goods extremely rewarding.

Galeries Lafayette New York (4–10 E. 57th St., tel. 212/355–0022). This new branch of the French fashion store, occupying the former site of Bonwit Teller, carries mostly French labels in an upscale assortment of better and designer apparel. Styles here tend more toward youthful than classic.

Henri Bendel (712 5th Ave., between 55th and 56th Sts., tel. 212/247–1100). Now firmly established under its beautiful new roof (having moved from West 57th Street), Bendel's continues to delight with its stylish displays and sophisticated little boutiques.

Lord & Taylor (424 5th Ave., between 38th and 39th Sts., tel. 212/391–3344). This store can be relied upon for the wearable, the fashionable, and the classic in clothes and accessories for women. It's refined, well-stocked and never overwhelming.

Macy's (Herald Sq., Broadway at 34th St., tel. 212/695–4400). No less than a miracle on 34th Street, Macy's main store is the largest retail store in America and, despite recent financial woes, is very much in business. Over the past two decades, it has grown chic enough to rival Bloomingdale's in the style department, but its main floor is reassuringly traditional. And for cooking gear and housewares, the Cellar nearly outdoes Zabar's, with which it has an annual year-end caviar price war.

Saks Fifth Avenue (611 5th Ave., between 49th and 50th Sts., tel. 212/753–4000). This wonderful store still embodies the spirit of service and style with which it opened in 1926. Saks believes in good manners, the ceremonies of life, and dressing for the part; the selection for men, women, and children—now doubled by recent expansion—reflects this quality.

Specialty Shops

Antiques   Many small dealers cluster in two antiques "malls":

Manhattan Art & Antiques Center (1050 2nd Ave., between 55th and 56th Sts., tel. 212/355–4400). More than 100 dealers stocking everything from paisley and Judaica to satsuma, scientifica, and samovars jumble the three floors here. The level of quality is not, as a rule, up to that of Madison Avenue, but then neither are the prices.

Place des Antiquaires (125 E. 57th St., tel. 212/758–2900). From its 30-foot-high marble-paved entrance to its glittering glass-walled shops, this is a lavish place. Its dealers offer such high-end goods as 17th-century tapestries, export porcelain, American folk art, and Chinese textiles.

Books   With so many of the country's publishing houses, magazines, and writers based here, there is an abundance of book shops, small and large. Of course, all the big national chains are here—Barnes & Noble, B. Dalton, Brentano's, Doubleday, Waldenbooks—with branches all over town.

Biography Bookshop (400 Bleecker St., tel. 212/807–8655). Diaries, letters, and other biographical and autobiographical material from small and large publishers worldwide fill this tidy, well-organized store.

Books & Company (939 Madison Ave., between 74th and 75th Sts., tel. 212/737–1450). A comfy sofa invites lingering here.

Coliseum Books (1771 Broadway at 57th St., tel. 212/757–8381). This supermarket of a bookstore has a huge, quirky selection of remainders, best-sellers, and scholarly works. Its late hours are worth knowing about.

Endicott Booksellers (450 Columbus Ave., between 81st and 82nd Sts., tel. 212/787–6300). This intelligent, wood-paneled bookstore features evening readings.

Gotham Book Mart (41 W. 47th St., tel. 212/719–4448). The late Frances Steloff opened this store years ago with just $200 in her pocket, half of it on loan. But she helped launch D. H. Lawrence and Henry Miller and is now legendary among bibliophiles, as is her bookstore, an oasis for those who truly love to read. Solid fiction and nonfiction are emphasized in the collection of nearly a quarter of a million books and 50,000 magazines. Though organization may seem haphazard, the knowledgeable staff can help you find what you want.

Rizzoli (31 W. 57th St., tel. 212/759–2424; 454 West Broadway, tel. 212/674–1616; World Financial Center, tel. 212/385–1400). An elegant marble entrance, oak paneling, chandeliers, and classical music accompany a stock of records and books on art, architecture, dance, design, foreign language, and travel uptown; the selection downtown, strong on business and children's titles, comes without the fin-de-siècle frills.

Shakespeare & Company (2259 Broadway at 81st St., tel. 212/580–7800). The stock here represents what's happening in publishing today in just about every field. Late hours are a plus.

Crystal Three peerless sources are **Baccarat** (625 Madison Ave., between 58th and 59th Sts., tel. 212/826–4100); **Hoya Crystal Gallery** (450 Park Ave., between 56th and 57th Sts., tel. 212/223–6335); and **Steuben** (715 5th Ave. at 56th St., tel. 212/752–1441).

Food **Balducci's** (424 6th Ave. at 9th St., tel. 212/673–2600). In this former mom-and-pop food shop, now one of the city's finest food stores, mounds of baby carrots keep company with frilly lettuce, feathery dill, and superlative meats, fish, cheeses, chocolates, baked goods, pastas, vinegars, oils, crackers, and prepared foods.

Dean & DeLuca (560 Broadway at Prince St., tel. 212/431–1691). This huge SoHo trendsetter, splendidly bright white, has an encyclopedic selection, from the heady array at the cheese counter to the shelves of crackers and the display cases of prepared foods.

Zabar's (2245 Broadway at 80th St., tel. 212/787–2000). Visit here not so much to snap up everything in sight—Zabar's now sells by mail order, too—as to enjoy the atmosphere of one of New York's favorite feeding troughs. Dried herbs and spices, dried fruits, chocolates, and assorted bottled foods are downstairs, along with a fragrant jumble of fresh breads and the cheese, meat, and smoked-fish counters. Upstairs is one of New York's largest selections of kitchenware.

Gizmos and Whatchamacallits

Hammacher Schlemmer (147 E. 57th St., tel. 212/421–9000). The store that offered America the first pop-up toaster, the first automatic steam iron, and the first telephone answering machine and microwave oven still ferrets out the outrageous, the unusual, and the best-of-kind.

Sharper Image (Pier 17, South St. Seaport, tel. 212/693–0477; 4 W. 57th St., tel. 212/265–2550). This retail outlet of the catalogue company stocks gifts for the pampered executive who has everything.

Jewelry, Watches, and Silver

Most of the world's premier jewelers have retail outlets in New York, and the nation's jewelry wholesale center is on 47th Street.

A La Vieille Russie (781 5th Ave., between 59th and 60th Sts., tel. 212/752–1727). Stop here to behold, up close, bibelots by Fabergé and others, encrusted with jewels or exquisitely enameled.

Buccellati (725 5th Ave., between 56th and 57th Sts. in Trump Tower, tel. 212/308–5533). The oversize Italian jewelry here makes a statement. Silver is around the corner (46 E. 57th St., tel. 212/308–2507).

Bulgari (730 5th Ave. at 57th St., tel. 212/315–9000, and 2 E. 61st St., in the Pierre Hotel, tel. 212/486–0086). The expertly crafted jewelry here has an understated, tailored look.

Cartier (2 E. 52nd St., tel. 212/753–0111). Simple but superb pieces are displayed in the former mansion of the late yachtsman and society king Morton F. Plant.

Tiffany & Co. (727 5th Ave. at 57th St., tel. 212/755–8000). A shiny robin's-egg-blue box from this venerable New York jeweler announces the contents as something very special. Along with the $50,000 platinum-and-diamond bracelets, there is a great deal that's affordable on a whim. **Van Cleef & Arpels** (744 5th Ave. at 57th St., tel. 212/644–9500). The jewelry here is sheer perfection.

Luggage and Leather Goods

Bottega Veneta (635 Madison Ave., between 59th and 60th Sts., tel. 212/319–0303). The superb goods here are for people who know real quality.

Crouch & Fitzgerald (400 Madison Ave. at 48th St., tel. 212/755–5888). Since 1839, this store has offered a terrific selection in hard- and soft-sided luggage, plus handbags.

Menswear

Brooks Brothers (346 Madison Ave. at 44th St., tel. 212/682–8800). The bare travertine underfoot, high ceilings overhead, and undecorated showcases on the ground floor suggest a New England spareness at this institution in American menswear. Styles are conservative, and tailoring standards are extremely high—as they have always been.

Frank Stella Ltd. (440 Columbus Ave. at 81st St., tel. 212/877–5566; 1382 6th Ave., between 56th and 57th Sts., tel. 212/757–2295). Classic clothing with subtle variations is offered here.

Paul Smith (108 5th Ave. at 16th St., tel. 212/627–9770). Dark mahogany Victorian cases display downtown styles.

Paul Stuart (Madison Ave. at 45th St., tel. 212/682–0320). In this celebrated retailer, the fabric selection is interesting, the tailoring superb, and the look traditional but not stodgy.

Saint Laurie, Ltd. (897 Broadway, between 19th and 20th Sts., tel. 212/473–0100). This family-owned business sells suits manufactured on the premises in styles ranging from the boxy to the Italianate in lovely fabrics. Prices are lower than for comparable garments elsewhere, but still not cheap.

Toys

Enchanted Forest (85 Mercer St., tel. 212/925–6677). Fancy reigns in this shop's stock of unique handmades.

F.A.O. Schwarz (767 5th Ave. at 58th St., tel. 212/644–9400). You will be hooked on this sprawling two-level children's store from the minute you walk through the door and one of the costumed staff members—a donkey, a clown, a cave woman, or a mad scientist—extends a welcome. In front of you is a wonderful mechanical clock with many dials and dingbats; beyond are all the stuffed animals in the world, dolls large and small, things to build with (including blocks by the pound), things to play dress-up with, computer things, games, toy cars (including a multi-thousand-dollar Ferrari), and much more.

Penny Whistle Toys (132 Spring St., tel. 212/925–2088; 448 Columbus Ave., between 81st and 82nd Sts., tel. 212/873–9090; 1283 Madison Ave., between 91st and 92nd Sts., tel. 212/369–3868). Meredith Brokaw, wife of newscaster Tom Brokaw, has developed an intriguing selection of quality toys here.

West Side Kids (498 Amsterdam Ave. at 84th St., tel. 212/496–7282). The shrewd selection here mixes educational toys with a grab bag of fun little playthings.

Women's Clothing
The department stores' collections are always good: **Saks** for its designers; **Macy's** for its breadth; **Bloomingdale's** for its extremes; **Barneys** for its trendy chic; and **Lord & Taylor** for its classicism. The following add another dimension.

Trendsetters
Charivari (2315 Broadway, between 83rd and 84th Sts., tel. 212/873–1424). Since Selma Weiser founded this store on the Upper West Side, she has made a name for herself internationally for her eagle eye on the up-and-coming and avant-garde. The branches, too, take a high-style, if pricey, approach: **Charivari Sport** (201 W. 79th St., tel. 212/799–8650); **Charivari Workshop** (441 Columbus Ave. at 81st St., tel. 212/496–8700); **Charivari 72** (257 Columbus Ave. at 72nd St., tel. 212/787–7272); and **Charivari 57** (18 W. 57th St., tel. 212/333–4040).

Patricia Field (10 E. 8th St., tel. 212/254–1699). This store collects the essence of the downtown look.

La Rue des Rêves (578 Broadway, tel. 212/226–6736). Stylish clothing for stylish women who like either an elegant, understated look or Tina Turner styles.

Designer Showcases
Alaïa New York (131 Mercer St., tel. 212/941–1166). The Paris-based designer shows his body-conscious clothing here.

Betsey Johnson (130 Thompson St., tel. 212/ 420–0169; 248 Columbus Ave., between 71st and 72nd Sts., tel. 212/362–3364). The look here is still hip.

Chanel (5 E. 57th St., tel. 212/355–5050). The classic designs here never go out of style.

Emanuel Ungaro (803 Madison Ave., between 67th and 68th Sts., tel. 212/249–4090). The style here is body-conscious, but it's never flashy.

Emporio Armani (110 5th Ave., between 16th and 17th Sts., tel. 212/727–3240). The Italian designer's casual line is featured.

Geoffrey Beene (783 5th Ave. at 59th St., tel. 212/935–0470). A splendid-looking boutique houses exquisite day and evening wear by America's master designer.

Giorgio Armani (815 Madison Ave., between 67th and 68th Sts., tel. 212/988–9191). In this lofty blond-and-beige space with grand, arched windows and doors, Armani's high-end line looks oh-so-chic.

Givenchy (954 Madison Ave. at 75th St., tel. 212/ 772–1040). This designer is famous for timeless elegance.

Hermès (11 E. 57th St., tel. 212/751–3181). Patterned scarves and Grace Kelly bags are hallmarks.

Missoni (836 Madison Ave. at 69th St., tel. 212/ 517–9339). Wonderfully textured knits, suits, and sportswear stand out.

Norma Kamali O.M.O. (11 W. 56th St., tel. 212/ 957–9797). The look here ranges from sweatshirts to evening gowns.

Polo/Ralph Lauren (867 Madison Ave. at 72nd St., tel. 212/606–2100). Lauren's flagship store is not only the ultimate expression of the Ralph Lauren way of life, it's also one of New York's most distinctive shopping experiences, in a grand, carefully renovated turn-of-the-century town house.

Sonia Rykiel (792 Madison Ave., at 67th St., tel. 212/744–0880). Signature knits for day and evening pack the racks.

Valentino (825 Madison Ave., between 68th and 69th Sts., tel. 212/744–0200). The mix here is at once audacious and beautifully cut, with the best of France and Italy on its racks.

Yves St. Laurent Rive Gauche (855 Madison Ave., between 70th and 71st Sts., tel. 212/988–

3821). The looks range from chic to classic for
day and evening.

Classicists **Ann Taylor** (2017 Broadway, near 69th St., tel.
212/873–7344; 25 Fulton St., tel. 212/608–5600;
805 3rd Ave. at 50th St., tel. 212/308–5333; 3 E.
57th St., tel. 212/832–2010 and other locations).
These stores provide what the elegant young
woman with a sense of style needs for work and
play; the Third Avenue location in particular
has excellent sales.
Burberry's (9 E. 57th St., tel. 212/371–5010).
The look is classic and conservative—and no-
body does a better trench coat.

Hip Styles **Canal Jean** (504 Broadway, between Spring and
Broome Sts., tel. 212/226–1130). Casual funk
draws hip shoppers.
Reminiscence (74 5th Ave., between 13th and
14th Sts., tel. 212/243–2292). The theme is
strictly '50s and '60s, in vintage and new clothing.
A/E (568 Broadway near Prince St., tel. 212/
431–6000). Here's Giorgio Armani's answer to
the Gap—with a sleek European touch and a
higher price tag.

Vintage **Harriet Love** (412 West Broadway, tel. 212/966–
2280). This is the doyenne of the city's vintage
clothing scene.
Screaming Mimi's (22 E. 4th St., tel. 212/677–
6464). Old clothes go avant-garde here.

4 Dining

With more than 16,000 restaurants (if you count coffeeshops and diners), New York has no lack of places to eat. At the top of the list are world-famous gourmet shrines with astronomical prices; at the humbler end of the spectrum are thousands of hole-in-the-walls, serving a variety of ethnic cuisines. The following list is a mere sampling, covering a range of prices, neighborhoods, and cuisines.

With the recession, New York's latest trend has been toward more casual, moderately-priced restaurants, but prices here are still well above most other cities. If you are intent on trying at least one top restaurant, bring your costs down by going at lunch instead of dinner, or by opting for a prix-fixe menu. And wherever you eat, when the waiter starts reciting specials, don't be shy about asking the price of a dish.

Reservations are always a good idea, for any restaurant that accepts them. Dress is generally casual (though not sloppy) unless a restaurant requires men to wear jackets and/or tie (reviews below specify where that's the case). A 15%–20% tip is standard; a quick way to figure how much to leave is to double the 8¼% tax charged on your bill.

Category	Cost*
Very Expensive	over $60
Expensive	$40–$60
Moderate	$20–$40
Inexpensive	under $20

per person, excluding drinks, service, and sales tax(8¼%)

The following credit card abbreviations are used: AE, American Express; DC, Diners Club; MC, MasterCard; and V, Visa. Highly recommended restaurants are indicated by a star (★).

Lower Manhattan

Expensive **Windows on the World.** 107 stories up, this restaurant boasts a peerless 55-mile view. The menu features American and international cui-

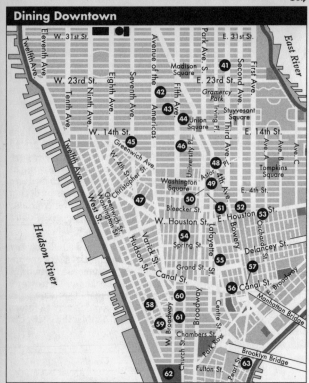

Dining Downtown

Acme Bar and Grill, **51**

Bayamo, **50**

Benito's II, **55**

Bouley, **59**

Bridge Cafe, **63**

Café de Bruxelles, **45**

Gotham Bar & Grill, **46**

Indochine, **49**

John's Pizzeria, **47**

Katz's Delicatessen, **53**

La Colombe d'Or, **41**

Lox Around the Clock, **42**

Montrachet, **60**

Odeon, **61**

Silver Palace, **57**

Siracusa Gourmet Café, **48**

SoHo Kitchen and Bar, **54**

TriBeCa Grill, **58**

Union Square Café, **44**

Windows on the World, **62**

Wong Kee, **56**

Yonah Schimmel's Knishery, **52**

Zip City Brewery, **43**

Dining Uptown

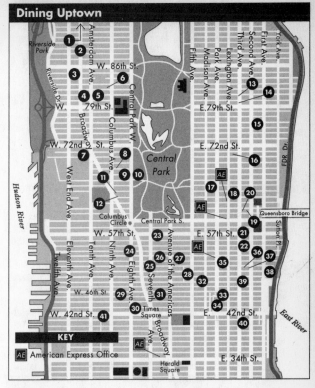

American
Festival Café, **28**
Amsterdam's, **4**
Anatolia, **13**
Arizona 206, **19**
Bangkok
Cuisine, **24**
Cabana
Carioca, **31**
Café des
Artistes, **9**

Café
Luxembourg, **7**
Chez
Josephine, **41**
China Grill, **27**
Dawat, **21**
Dock's, **2, 40**
E.J.'s
Luncheonette, **5**
Fiorello's Roman
Café, **12**
Four Seasons, **35**
Ginger Man, **11**
Grand Central
Oyster Bar, **34**
Hatsuhana,
32, 33

JoJo, **18**
Le Bernadin, **25**
Le Cirque, **17**
Luke's Bar &
Grill, **14**
Lutèce, **36**
Ollie's Noodle
Shop, **1, 3, 30**
Orso, **29**
P.J. Clarke's, **22**
Poiret, **6**
Remi, **26**

Russian Tea
Room, **23**
Sette Mezzo, **16**
Smith &
Wollensky, **39**
Tavern on the
Green, **10**
Vasata, **15**
Vince &
Eddie's, **8**
Wylie's Ribs &
Co., **38**
Yellowfingers, **20**
Zarela, **37**

sine; the wine list is superlative. To enjoy the same views with drinks or a light nosh, there's the adjacent Hors d'Oeuvrerie. *1 World Trade Center, tel. 212/938–1111. Reservations required. Jacket and tie required. AE, DC, MC, V.*

Moderate **Bridge Café.** Named after the Brooklyn Bridge (which looms overhead), this wood-frame café built in 1801 has a bit more authentic atmosphere than the restaurants in the nearby South Street Seaport mall. The small but lively menu is strong on salads and seafood. *279 Water St. (at Dover St.), tel. 212/227–3344. Reservations advised. AE, DC, MC, V.*

SoHo and TriBeCa

Very Expensive ★ **Bouley.** Owner-chef David Bouley's creative dishes have won this elegant downtown spot a top reputation, so reserve well in advance and be patient with the slow service once you're there—it could be the best meal you'll ever eat. The constantly-changing menu leans toward fresh fish and game; the hot chocolate dessert soufflé is justifiably famous. *165 Duane St. (near Hudson St.), tel. 212/608–3852. Reservations required. Jacket and tie required. AE, DC, MC, V. Closed Sat. lunch and Sun.*

Expensive **Montrachet.** Though you'll be in gritty-chic TriBeCa, the ambience in this chummy, casual restaurant is backstreet Paris—wood tables with white cloths, dusty-rose-colored banquettes. The full-flavored Provençal cooking is strong on fresh fish (black sea bass, lobster, red snapper) and fowl (pheasant, guinea hen). *239 W. Broadway (near White St.), tel. 212/219–2777. Reservations advised. AE. Closed Sun.; dinner only, except for Fri. lunch.*

Moderate **Odeon.** In this converted Art Deco cafeteria, a neighborhood pioneer, TriBeCa's artsy chic was first defined. The cooking is still top-quality—both French brasserie-style (steak and frites) or American fare. *145 W. Broadway (at Thomas St.), tel. 212/233–0507. Reservations advised. AE, DC, MC, V. Closed Sat. lunch.*

★ **TriBeCa Grill.** Installed in a cavernous space of exposed brick and pipes, this is a celebrity hotspot—its owners include Robert DeNiro and Mikhail Baryshnikov. Despite its hipness, every customer is treated warmly and the food is first-rate: veal chops, lobster, wonderful potato pancakes. Don't miss the ornate bar, a relic of the late Maxwell's Plum uptown. *375 Greenwich St. (near Franklin St.), tel. 212/941–3900. Reservations advised. AE, DC, MC, V. Closed Sat. lunch.*

Inexpensive SoHo Kitchen and Bar. The city's biggest cruvinet serves 96 different wines by the glass—and 14 champagnes—at this lofty-ceilinged brick-walled charmer. Pastas and pizzas star. *103 Greene St. (between Prince and Spring Sts.), tel. 212/925–1866. Reservations advised for 6 or more; no reservations Sat. dinner. AE, DC, MC, V.*

Chinatown, Little Italy, and the Lower East Side

These three ethnic neighborhoods offer the kinds of authentic dining experiences that transplanted New Yorkers miss most. Not all restaurants take credit cards, but at these prices, you can afford to pay cash. The narrow streets of Chinatown, particularly **Mott, Bayard,** and **Pell** streets, are a cornucopia of Chinese restaurants; every New Yorker claims to know the "best," but you can almost pick one at random and get a good meal. Along Little Italy's **Mulberry Street,** heady aromas of garlic and oil may tempt you into any of a dozen restaurants. The Lower East Side, an old Jewish immigrant neighborhood, is a bit harder to penetrate, but if you love Kosher-style cooking, don't pass it up.

Moderate Benito's II. One of the few in Little Italy to accept reservations, this restaurant, with exposed brick walls, tile murals, a dark wood ceiling, and small tables neatly covered in white linen, offers substantial fare pungently laced with garlic. *163 Mulberry St. (near Broome St.), tel. 212/226–9012. Reservations advised. No credit cards.*

Inexpensive **Katz's Delicatessen.** At this century-old deli, the noise level can be a bit much, but so are the portions, so come hungry. Classics include knishes, pastrami, brisket, and fat garlicky pickles; the corned beef is a must. Waiting in line is part of the scene. *205 E. Houston St. (near Orchard St.), tel. 212/254–2246. Reservations unnecessary. AE.*

Silver Palace. The draw here on weekends is dim sum, a parade of dishes wheeled around the second-floor dining room on carts that stop at each table for diners to sample from. Be adventurous and fill your plate with anything from exotic curried squid to delectable dumplings. *52 Bowery (near Canal St.), tel. 212/964–1204. Reservations accepted. AE, DC, MC, V.*

Wong Kee. Behind this unassuming brushed-metal facade, you can count on low-priced, high-quality Cantonese fare. Highlights include barbecued pork, spiced beef chow fun (wide rice noodles), or sweet-and-pungent chicken (a refinement of sweet-and-sour). *113 Mott St. (near Canal St.), tel. 212/226–9018. No reservations. No credit cards. BYOB.*

Yonah Schimmel's Knishery. Crisp, golden knishes—dough pockets stuffed with anything from potatoes to fruits and cheese—are the star attraction at this long-established Lower East Side spot. *137 E. Houston St. (near 2nd Ave.), tel. 212/477–2858. Reservations unnecessary. No credit cards.*

Greenwich Village

While the West Village has its share of expensive gourmet restaurants, the Village dining experience is best characterized by unpretentious shopfront restaurants, many of them ethnic, that have been pleasing locals for decades. Streets to prowl for authentic, inexpensive meals are **Second and First avenues** between 10th and 6th streets, where Polish and Ukrainian coffeeshops alternate with trendy artist/student bars, and **6th Street** between First and Second avenues, where there's a great line-up of Indian restaurants.

Expensive **Gotham Bar and Grill.** Like its namesake, this
★ Gotham is huge, crowded, and sophisticated. The decor is strikingly postmodern, the menu

eclectic. Serious gourmands flock here for dishes such as roasted quail salad, grilled loin of rabbit, or penne with wild mushrooms. *12 E. 12th St. (near 5th Ave.), tel. 212/620–4020. Reservations recommended. Jacket advised. AE, DC, MC, V. Closed lunch weekends.*

Moderate **Café de Bruxelles.** Hearty French and Belgian dishes—juicy boudin blanc, tangy choucroute, and waterzooi fish stew—are the specialties at this lace-curtained brasserie with a zinc-topped bar. The french fries are crisply terrific. *118 Greenwich Ave. (at 13th St.), tel. 212/206–1830. Reservations accepted. AE, DC, MC, V. Closed Mon.*

Indochine. Across the street from the Public Theater, this large, airy space with an artsy clientele serves up exotically spiced Vietnamese and Cambodian specialties. After spring roll appetizers, best bets include stuffed boneless chicken wings or marinated beef salad. *430 Lafayette St. (near Astor Pl.), tel. 212/505–5111. Reservations advised. AE, DC, MC, V. Dinner only.*

Siracusa Gourmet Café. Country-style Sicilian recipes geared for sophisticated palates are served in this unassuming spot. Mixed antipasti is a treat, as are any of the creative pastas and creamy *gelati* (Italian ice creams). *65 4th Ave. (near 10th St.), tel. 212/254–1940. Reservations advised. AE. Closed Sat. lunch and Sun.*

Inexpensive **Acme Bar and Grill.** This narrow, noisy joint, with its mismatched chairs, wood tables, and exposed-brick walls, serves heaping plates of down-home southern cooking. There's plenty of seafood—plump fried oysters and farm-raised catfish—as well as delicious corn fritters, Cajun peanut soup, and an incredibly rich chocolate mud pie. *9 Great Jones St. (near Broadway), tel. 212/420–1934. No reservations. DC, MC, V.*

Bayamo. In this brightly-colored loft with cast-iron columns, a noisy, fun atmosphere reigns. Be adventurous when you order; the menu features Cuban-Chinese peasant food such as *ropa vieja* (Cuban pot roast). *704 Broadway (near 4th St.). tel. 212/475–5151. Reservations advised. AE, DC, MC, V.*

★ **John's Pizzeria.** It's hard to find better pizza
than the thin-crusted pies baked here in coal-
fired brick ovens. John's looks just like what it
is—an unpretentious neighborhood pizza parlor
that's been around for half a century—but locals
swear by it. *278 Bleecker St. (between 6th and
7th Aves.), tel. 212/243-1680. No reservations.
No credit cards.*

Chelsea, Flatiron District, and Gramercy Park

Moderate **La Colombe D'Or.** At this cozy, lace-curtained
basement spot, the cooking goes well beyond
standard French bistro fare: seared sea scal-
lops, succulent calves' liver, grilled duck, alongside some tasty specials from the chef's native
Tangiers. *134 E. 26th St., tel. 212/689-0666.
Reservations advised. AE, DC, MC, V. Closed
weekend lunch.*

Union Square Café. Blond wood floors and
cream-colored walls splashed with bright murals create a warm, airy setting for chef Michael
Romano's innovative cooking. Appetizers include the signature Oysters Union Square; entrees may include grilled marinated tuna or
roast loin of rabbit. Don't pass up the hot garlic
potato chips. *21 E. 16th St., tel. 212/243-4020.
Reservations advised. AE, DC, MC, V. Closed
Sun. lunch.*

Inexpensive **Lox Around the Clock.** Traditional deli favorites
such as bagels with lox (smoked salmon),
blintzes, or borscht (beet soup), are served up
along with burgers and thick-stuffed sandwiches. A blaring jukebox and funky decor—
battered plaster walls and pendant fluorescent
tubes—add to the spirit. *676 6th Ave. (at 21st
St.), tel. 212/691-3535. Reservations unnecessary. AE.*

Zip City Brewery. Manhattan's only micro-
brewery features two gleaming copper brewing
tanks towering over the polished, inlaid bar. Ac-
companying the excellent ales, beers, and lagers
is American food with a twist; you can also get a
good basic burger here. *3 W. 18th St., tel. 212/
366-6333. Reservations accepted for six or
more. AE, DC, MC, V.*

Midtown East

Very Expensive

Four Seasons. This landmark restaurant in the Seagram Building has two dining rooms—the flower-bedecked Pool Rom and the rosewood Grill Room, site of power lunches. The imaginative and unpredictable menu puts an Oriental spin on traditional American and French cuisine; roast duck and rack of lamb are reliable choices. The famous Spa Cuisine menu allows you to splurge without lots of calories. *99 E. 52nd St., tel. 212/754–9494. Reservations required. Jacket and tie required. AE, DC, MC, V. Closed Sat. lunch and Sun.*

★ **Lutèce.** Over the years, chef/owner André Soltner has turned this intimate midtown town house into a temple of classic French gastronomy. The regular menu is varied, and specials change daily; grilled trout and pheasant are always fine choices. Service is attentive and impeccable. *249 E. 50th St., tel. 212/752–2225. Reservations required. Jacket and tie required. AE, DC, MC, V. Closed Sun. and Aug.; dinner only on Mon. and Sat.*

Expensive

Grand Central Oyster Bar. Down in the catacombs beneath Grand Central Terminal, the Oyster Bar has a reputation for serving ultrafresh seafood. The vast main room is usually crowded at lunch; solos can sit at the counter, and there's a clubby rear room as well. Besides a dozen varieties of oysters, there are delicious chowders, fish stews, and grilled fillets. *Grand Central Terminal, tel. 212/490–6650. Lunch reservations required, dinner reservations advised. AE, DC, MC, V. Closed weekends.*

★ **Smith & Wollensky.** One of the best of the midtown steak houses, Smith & Wollensky serves big blackened sirloins and filets mignons with pepper sauce, as well as huge lobsters, veal chops, and onion rings. The wine list is extraordinary, the atmosphere masculine. *201 E. 49th St., tel. 212/753–1530. Reservations advised. AE, DC, MC, V. Main restaurants closed weekend lunch.*

Moderate

Dock's. Like its Upper West Side sibling (*see below*), the midtown Dock's serves delicious fresh seafood—grilled salmon and tuna, oysters and clams, and some of the best crab cakes in town.

The decor is a sophisticated replica of an old-time seafood house. *633 3rd Ave. (at 40th St.), tel. 212/986–8080. Reservations advised. AE, DC, MC, V.*

Hatsuhana. Visiting Japanese businessmen come here for ultra-fresh sushi and sashimi, as well as bite-sized fried crabs, grilled teriyaki fish, and other Japanese specialties. *237 Park Ave. (on 46th St.), tel. 212/661–3400; 17 E. 48th St., tel. 212/355–3345. Reservations required. Jacket and tie advised. AE, DC, MC, V. Closed Sat. lunch and Sun.*

Zarela. Refined Mexican cuisine is served beneath festive piñatas and crêpe-paper streamers. No greasy burritos here: The menu features light-seasoned *fajitas* (skirt steak), *salpicon* (red snapper), and tuna with mole sauce. *953 2nd Ave. (near 50th St.), tel. 212/644–6740. Reservations advised. AE, DC. Closed weekend lunch.*

Inexpensive **P. J. Clarke's.** This venerable tile-floored saloon doesn't look much different now than it did in the 1944 movie *The Lost Weekend.* Skip the singles scene at the crowded bar and head for the back room for decent burgers, chili, salads, and home fries. *915 3rd Ave. (at 55th St.), tel. 212/759–1650. Reservations advised. AE, DC, MC, V.*

Wylie's Ribs & Co. Here's an essential stop for anyone who loves barbecued ribs and chicken, which are served here by the platterful. *891 1st Ave (at 50th St.), tel. 212/751–0700. Reservations advised. AE, DC, MC, V.*

Theater District

If you're heading for a Broadway show, try any of the restaurants along 46th Street between 8th and 9th avenues, a block known as **Restaurant Row.** Price ranges vary, but most of these restaurants are quite reliable—and their staffs are skilled at getting diners out in time for an 8 o'clock curtain. If classic delis are more to your taste, go to **7th Avenue** between 54th and 55th streets, and choose between long-standing rivals the Carnegie Deli and the Stage Deli, both serving garantuan sandwiches with all the trappings.

Very Expensive **Le Bernardin.** The New York branch of an illustrious Paris seafood house occupies the ground floor of the Equitable Assurance Tower. Decor is corporate and elegant; the menu teems with ocean treasures, such as roasted monkfish or *rouelle* of salmon. *155 W. 51st St., tel. 212/489–1515. Reservations required. Jacket and tie required. AE, DC, MC, V. Closed Sun.*

Expensive **Russian Tea Room.** Next door to Carnegie Hall, this is a major New York scene, loaded with media people (Dustin Hoffman lunched here with his agent in *Tootsie*). Even if you're seated on the celebrity-less second floor, you can feast on borscht (beet soup), blini with caviar, and chicken Kiev. Jacques Pepin is a consulting chef here. *150 W. 57th St., tel. 212/265–0947. Reservations advised. Jacket required at dinner. AE, DC, MC, V.*

Moderate ★ **American Festival Café.** Set beside Rockefeller Center's lower plaza (skating rink in winter, open-air café in summer), this fine restaurant serves American regional classics, with a folk-art inspired decor to match. Try the crab cakes or the prime rib. The pretheater dinner is a good value. *20 W. 50th St., tel. 212/246–6699. Reservations advised. AE, DC, MC, V.*

Chez Josephine. Amid the Off-Broadway theaters of Theater Row, this 1920's-style bistro evokes the Parisian milieu of the owner's second mother, Josephine Baker. Entreés include roast quail and lobster cassoulet. *414 W. 42nd St., tel. 212/594–1925. Reservations advised. AE, MC, V. Closed Sun. and lunch.*

China Grill. This sleek, minimalist restaurant on the ground floor of the CBS Building serves a French-American menu with Oriental accents, an assortment of grilled dishes with emphasis on fish. Very popular, it can be noisy. *52 W. 53rd St., tel. 212/333–7788. Reservations advised. Jacket advised. AE, DC, MC, V. Closed weekend lunch.*

★ **Remi.** Northern Italian cuisine stars here, beneath Venetian glass chandeliers and a huge mural of the Grand Canal. Esepecially delicious is the daily risotto special. *145 W. 53rd St., tel. 212/581–4242. Reservations advised. AE, DC, MC, V. Closed weekend lunch.*

Orso. Reserve well ahead to get into this popular

Theater Row spot, where you'll probably glimpse a celebrity or two. Lively pastas and thin-crust pizzas with zesty toppings are the fundamentals of the changing menu. *322 W. 46th St., tel. 212/489-7212. Reservations accepted 1 wk in advance only. MC, V.*

Inexpensive **Bangkok Cuisine.** Just north of the Theater District is one of the city's best Thai restaurants. Order a Thai beer to accompany steamed fish, *pad thai* (a peanut and noodle dish), or crispy mee krob noodles. *885 8th Ave. (near 53rd St.), tel. 212/581-6370. Reservations advised. AE, MC, V. Closed Sun. lunch.*

Cabana Carioca. Climb a flight of stairs to sample the best Brazilian food in New York. Black beans, *feijoada* (savory meat stew), and seafood are cooked with a blend of Portuguese, Indian, and West African flavors. *123 W. 45th St., tel. 212/581-8088. Reservations advised. AE, DC, MC, V.*

Upper East Side

Very Expensive ★ **Le Cirque.** Elegant decor, superb service, and a clientele of beautiful people help to place Le Cirque at the acme of New York restaurants. The menu changes constantly, but its ambitious French-influenced choices usually include seafood, game, and pastas; the desserts are simply mouth-watering. *58 E. 65th St., tel. 212/794-9292. Reservations required. Jacket and tie required. AE, DC, MC, V. Closed Sun.*

Expensive **Arizona 206.** Southwestern decor—white plaster walls, raw timber trim, and piped-in Willie Nelson tunes—creates the setting for chili-flavored cuisine to match. Creative specials range from smoked-sturgeon quesadillas to lobster tostada salad. *206 E. 60th St., tel. 212/838-0440. Reservations advised. AE, DC, MC, V. Closed Sun. lunch.*

Moderate **Anatolia.** This postmodern exotic, with faux stone columns and crinkle-glazed pastel walls, offers Middle Eastern delights such as quail in vine leaves and lamb shanks in lemon sauce. The tasty hors d'oeuvres (*mezze*) can be a meal in themselves. *1422 3rd Ave. (between 80th and 81st Sts.), tel. 212/517-6262. Reservations advised. AE, DC, MC, V. Closed Sun. in Aug.*

Dawat. This softly-lit sophisticated Indian restaurant follows the recipes of actress-cookbook author Madhur Jaffrey, with savory and often spicy dishes, including several vegetarian specialties and robust breads. *210 E. 58th St., tel. 212/355–7555. Reservations advised. AE, DC, MC, V. Closed Sun. lunch.*

★ **JoJo.** Top chef Jean-Georges Vongherichten (previously at the Lafayette Restaurant) has brought his creative cooking to a new audience with this busy little moderate-priced bistro. *160 E. 64th St., tel. 212/223–5656. Reservations required. AE, MC, V. Closed Sun.*

Sette Mezzo. Among the profusion of Italian restaurants in this part of town, Sette Mezzo has justly earned its popularity. Like its uptown sibling, Vico Ristorante (on 2nd Avenue near 83rd Street), it turns fresh pasta, mozzarella, spicy sausage, and Italian vegetables (zucchini, broccoli rape) into marvelous trattoria dishes. *969 Lexington Ave. (near 70th St.), tel. 212/472–0400. Reservations required. No credit cards.*

Vašata. This cozy long-established Czech restaurant serves hearty meals of goulash, schnitzel, dumplings, and genuine Pilsner Urquell beer. The decor is homey, the service friendly. *339 E. 75th St., tel. 212/988–7166. Reservations advised. AE, MC, V. Closed Mon.*

Inexpensive **Luke's Bar & Grill.** A fairly new spot, with a young and affluent crowd of regulars, this wood-paneled neighborhood hang-out serves upscale (and very good) standards such as burgers, fries, spaghetti, soups, and salads. *1394 3rd Ave. (between 79th and 80th Sts), tel. 212/249–7070. Reservations advised for 6 or more. No credit cards.*

Yellowfingers. Convenient to Bloomingdale's and the Upper East side first-run movie houses, this is a reliable spot for a lively meal. Salads are a good bet, as is anything grilled. *200 E. 60th St., tel. 212/751–8615. No reservations. AE, DC, MC, V.*

Lincoln Center

Expensive **Café des Artistes.** With its sylvan murals and hushed atmosphere, this romantic restaurant serves country French food such as confit of duck and herb-crusted tuna steak. You won't want to rush your meal (the desserts are too good to skip), so come here after the ballet rather than before. *1 W. 67th St., tel. 212/877–3500. Reservations required. Jacket required at dinner. AE, DC, MC, V.*

Tavern on the Green. Set within Central Park, with wide windows looking out at constellations of tiny white lights, this special-occasion restaurant now boasts ex-Maxim's chef Marc Poidevin. Entrees include stuffed breast of veal with sage sauce and red snapper with fried leeks and shiitake mushrooms. *Central Park West at 67th St., tel. 212/873–3200. Reservations advised. AE, DC, MC, V.*

Moderate **Café Luxembourg.** The setting is Paris bistro, the buzzing crowd pure New York. Come here for well-honed brasserie stand-bys salted with nouvelle American ideas; baby lamb and filet mignon are good bets, as is the crème brûlée. *200 W. 70th St., tel. 212/873–7411. Reservations advised. AE, DC, MC, V. Dinner only except Sun. lunch.*

Fiorello's Roman Café. He-man veal chops and robust pastas top the menu at this cheerful, busy spot across the street from Lincoln Center (the staff is great at moving everyone out by curtain time). The pizzas are disappointing. *1900 Broadway (between 63rd and 64th Sts.), tel. 212/595–5330. Reservations advised. AE, MC, V.*

Inexpensive **The Ginger Man.** A warren of cozy rooms helps this busy saloon serve big pre-Lincoln Center crowds and weekend brunches. Besides standard burgers and salads, the menu has entrees such as rack of lamb or roast duck. *51 W. 64th St., tel. 212/874–5100. Reservations required. AE, DC, MC, V.*

★ **Vince & Eddie's.** Brick walls, oilcloth-covered tables, and a fireplace create a cozy setting for hearty fare like bean soup, onion tart, roast chicken, and mashed turnips. At this location and these prices, no wonder it's so popular. *70 W. 68th St., tel. 212/721–0068. Reservations advised. AE, DC, MC, V.*

> *This trip we found a road less traveled. And the perfect way to see it.*

©1992 Budget Rent a Car Corporation

Vacation Cars. Vacation Prices. Wherever you travel, Budget offers you a wide selection of quality cars – from economy models to roomy minivans and even convertibles. You'll find them all at competitively low rates that include unlimited mileage. At over 1500 locations in the U.S. and Canada. For information and reservations, call your travel consultant or Budget at **800-527-0700.** In Canada, call **800-268-8900.**

THE SMART MONEY IS ON BUDGET.®

Upper West Side

Moderate **Amsterdam's.** Behind the lively, crowded bar, the small dining room serves tasty food hot off the rotisserie (the chicken is delectable), as well as pastas, salads, and sandwiches. *428 Amsterdam Ave. (near 80th St.),, tel. 212/874–1377. No reservations. Dress: casual. AE, DC, MC, V.*

Dock's. As at its midtown sibling (see above), fresh seafood—raw, grilled, or artfully fried—is the specialty here. *2427 Broadway (near 89th St.), tel. 212/986–8080. Reservations advised. AE, DC, MC, V.*

★ **Poiret.** Behind the funky mosaic facade lies a noisy, somewhat cramped, but friendly dining room serving excellent bistro food. Filet mignon and steak bearnaise are good, accompanied by crisp fries; couscous dishes add a North African touch. *474 Columbus Ave. (between 82nd and 83rd Sts.), tel. 212/724–6880. Reservations advised. AE, DC, MC, V. Dinner only except Sun. lunch.*

Inexpensive **E. J.'s Luncheonette.** Decorated like a vintage diner, E.J.'s carries out the theme with a retro menu—breakfast waffles, soups, burgers, triple-decker sandwiches, and malteds—and low prices that seem from another era, too. It's popular, but worth the stand in line. *433 Amsterdam Ave. (near 80th St.), tel. 212/873–3444. No reservations. No credit cards.*

Ollie's Noodle Shop. At two locations—one across from the West Side's biggest multiplex cinema, the other up by Barnard and Columbia University—Ollie's serves a full menu of Chinese food, including some very good dumplings, noodles, and roast chicken. There are burgers, pasta, and sandwiches for Western palates, too. A third branch recently opened near Times Square. *2315 Broadway (at 84th St.), tel. 212/362–3712; 2957 Broadway (at 116th St.), tel. 212/932–3300; 190 W. 44th St., tel. 212/921–5988. No reservations. AE, MC, V.*

5 Lodging

By Jane
Hershey

*A New
York–based
freelance
writer whose
work has
appeared in*
Good
Housekeeping,
US, *and* Elle,
*Jane Hershey
is a long-time
contributor to
various
Fodor's
guides.*

If any single element of your trip to New York City is going to cost you a lot of money, it'll be your hotel bill. European cities may offer plenty of low-priced—albeit undistinguished—lodgings, but New York doesn't. Real estate is at a premium here, and labor costs are high, so hoteliers start out with a lot of expenses to cover. And there are enough well-heeled visitors to support competition at the premium end of the spectrum, which is where the profits are. Considering the healthy occupancy rate, market forces are not likely to drive current prices down. Fleabags and flophouses aside, there's precious little here for under $100 a night. We have noted a few budget properties, but on the sliding scale of Manhattan prices even our "Inexpensive" category includes hotels that run as high as $135 for one night's stay in a double room.

Once you've accepted that you must pay the going price, though, you'll have plenty of choices. In general, Manhattan hotels don't measure up to those in other U.S. cities in terms of room size, parking, or outside landscaping. But, this being a sophisticated city, New York hotels usually compensate with fastidious service, sprucely maintained properties, and restaurants that hold their own in a city of very knowledgeable diners.

Basic rules of decorum and dress are observed at the better hotels. With few exceptions, jackets (and frequently ties) are required in formal dining and bar areas after 5 or 6 PM. Bare feet or beach sandals are not allowed, and an overall sloppy appearance won't encourage good service.

Most Manhattan hotels are in the midtown area, so we have categorized them by price range rather than location. Exact prices could be misleading: Properties change their so-called "rack rates" seasonally, and most hotels offer weekend packages that include such tempting extras as complimentary meals, drinks, or tickets to events. Your travel agent may have brochures about such packages; also look for advertisements in travel magazines or the Sunday travel sections of major newspapers such as the *New*

York Times, the *Washington Post*, or the *Los Angeles Times*.

Highly recommended lodgings are indicated by a star ★.

Category	Cost*
Very Expensive	over $260
Expensive	$180–$260
Moderate	$135–$180
Inexpensive	under $135

All prices are for a standard double room, excluding 21¼% city and state sales tax.

The following credit card abbreviations are used: AE, American Express; DC, Diners Club; MC, MasterCard; V, Visa.

Unless otherwise noted in the individual descriptions, all the hotels listed have the following features and services: private baths, central heating, air-conditioning, private telephones, on-premises dining, valet and room service (though not necessarily 24-hour or short notice), TV (including cable and pay-per-view films), and a routine concierge staff.

Very Expensive

★ **The Carlyle.** Located in one of the city's finest residential areas, this beautifully appointed traditional hotel is considered one of New York's finest. The mood is English manor house; larger rooms and suites, many of them decorated by the famous interior designer Mark Hampton, have terraces, pantries, and antique furnishings. Baths, though more subdued than others in town, are marbled and chock-full of de rigueur amenities such as hair dryers, fine toiletries, and makeup mirrors. Most visitors have heard about the famous Café Carlyle, where performers such as Bobby Short entertain. But the hotel also contains the charming Bemelman's Bar, with whimsical animal murals on the walls and live piano music at night, and the formal Carlyle Restaurant, with French cuisine and old-fashioned courtly service. There's a

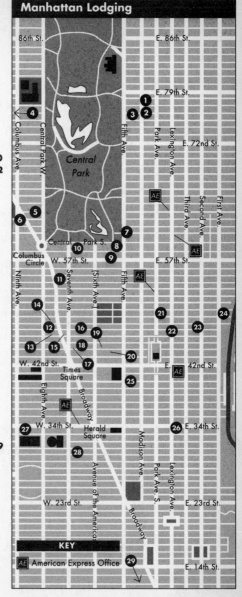

Manhattan Lodging

KEY

AE American Express Office

jewel of a fitness center that is ultraprivate and luxurious. This is one of the few grand hotels where European elegance and American friendliness really mix; you don't have to be a famous face to get a smile or good treatment. The concierge service is especially excellent. *35 E. 76th St., 10021, tel. 212/744–1600, fax 212/717–4682. 185 rooms. Facilities: restaurant, café, bar, lounge, VCRs and stereos, fax machines, kitchenettes and pantries in larger units, fitness center, meeting rooms. AE, DC, MC, V.*

★ **Essex House.** Hopes ran high when Japan's Nikko Hotels bought this stately Central Park South property, and the dream of turning around this fading, potentially grand hotel has certainly been realized. The public interiors are an Art Deco masterpiece fit for Fred and Ginger. The hotel's informal restaurant, Café Botanica, faces Central Park and resembles a lush prewar English greenhouse. Les Célébrités features the cuisine of Chef Christian Delouvrier, served in an intimate setting replete with surprisingly competent celebrity artwork from folks like Billy Dee Williams and James Dean. There is also a traditional Japanese restaurant. Journey's, the hotel's Hemingwayesque wood-paneled bar, has a working fireplace. The delights continue upstairs, where guest rooms and baths resemble those in a splendid English country home. Fabrics and furnishings are at once elegant and inviting. Many baths feature double sinks and separate stall showers. Guests staying in suites receive many complimentary extras such as garment and shoe bags (which can be taken home at no extra cost). The staff is discreet, efficient, and extremely friendly. This is the place to take advantage of weekend rates and book that dreamed-about double on the park; it won't break the bank as much as you might think. *160 Central Park South (near 7th Ave.), 10019, tel. 212/247–0300, fax 212/315–1839. 593 rooms. Facilities: 3 restaurants, bar, fitness center, meeting rooms, ballroom, business center. AE, DC, MC, V.*

The Mark. Just one block north of the Carlyle, the former Madison Avenue Hotel has recently been completely redone by its new owner, Rafael Hotels; it could provide its neighbor with some healthy competition in terms of price and amenities. Sadly, at press time some rooms were not up to previous standards. Ask to see your unit before checking in. Color schemes are warm to reflect the Italian neoclassical motif. Women will feel comfortable in the discreet public areas. Mark's, a cozy and elegant restaurant and lounge, features the unique French-American cuisine of chef Philippe Boulot. *25 E. 77th St., 10021, tel. 212/744–4300 or 800/843–6275, fax 212/744–2749. 185 rooms. Facilities: restaurant, café, lounge, meeting rooms, VIP suites with terraces. AE, DC, MC, V.*

★ **The Pierre.** The Four Seasons, a Canadian hotel group, has made a specialty of "freshening up" classic properties, and the Pierre is one of their notable successes. One might expect haughtiness along with the creamy, (recently spruced-up) oriental-carpeted halls and bright chandeliers, but you won't find that here: The staff has a sense of fun about working in these posh surroundings. Rooms, most of which have been recently refurbished, are traditionally decorated in soft floral patterns, with quilted bedspreads and fine wood furniture. Café Pierre can hold its own against many of the city's best spots; the Bar features low-key jazz piano in the evenings, and formal afternoon tea is served under the blue cherubim-filled dome of the Rotunda. There are no gimmicks here—just good old-fashioned style and service. *5th Ave. at 61st St., 10021, tel. 212/838–8000 or 800/332–3442, fax 212/940–8109. 204 rooms. Facilities: restaurant, bar, tearoom, meeting rooms, manned elevators, packing service upon request, hand-laundry service. AE, DC, MC, V.*

The Plaza. When real-estate developer and casino operator Donald Trump purchased this National Historic Landmark in 1988, locals shuddered a bit, but there is actually much to applaud. (Trump's fortunes have since waned, and by now The Plaza might be under new ownership.) This former haunt of F. Scott Fitzgerald, George M. Cohan, Frank Lloyd Wright, and the Beatles is ready to receive a relatively demanding public. Prices have edged up, but so has the quality of even the least expensive rooms. New color schemes are in burgundy or teal blue; fresh, floral-patterned quilted spreads grace the large beds. Furnishings, though still "hotel-like" in most units, are of high quality. Bathrooms, even those not yet fully redone, have fluffy new towels and toiletries. One real advantage here is the size of guest rooms—only a handful of other classic properties can offer similar spaciousness in nearly all accommodations. *5th Ave. at 59th St., 10019, tel. 212/759-3000 or 800/228-3000, fax 212/546-5324. 807 rooms. Facilities: 2 restaurants, 2 bars, café, art gallery, handicapped-guest rooms, meeting rooms, packing service upon request, large concierge staff. AE, DC, MC, V.*

Expensive

★ **Embassy Suites.** Another welcome addition to the Times Square area, this familiar name's new flagship has far more flair than anticipated. The elevated lobby is done up in modern art deco style; color schemes and furnishings are bold and contemporary. Suites have coffeemakers, small microwave ovens, refrigerators, and even complimentary sodas and snacks. Guest rooms, though hardly elegant, are cheerful and comfortable. Certain suites have been "child-proofed" with such safety features as bumpers placed over sharp edges. All rates include free full breakfast, and daily cocktails in a private lounge area. There's also a regular restaurant and bar, featuring well-priced grills and salads. A complete day-care center with trained staff is an added plus for families. Embassy will have to beef up its street-level security; the block continues to be somewhat unsavory. *1568 Broadway at 47th St., 10036, tel. 212/719-1600 or 800/ EMBASSY, fax 212/921-5212. 460 suites. Facilities: restaurant, bar, meeting rooms, day-care center, complimentary use of nearby health club and pool. AE, DC, MC, V.*

Hotel Macklowe. Real-estate magnate Harry Macklowe's answer to what savvy business travelers really want is right about on target. Though hard by Times Square, it has more elegance than other commercial hotels in the area. The lobby and dining areas are done in handsome, subdued art-deco style, with polished woods and rich carpets. There is a cozy bar and a boardroomish restaurant called Charlotte, which features notable though sometimes uneven American nouvelle cuisine. Guest rooms, though not oversize, are tasteful and well-appointed, and keep the working traveler in mind. The informed, friendly staff goes out of its way to encourage guests to enjoy a more leisurely pace and share the Big Apple with significant others and children. With competitive weekend rates, this hotel has also become a popular "sleeper" for visitors who want gracious surroundings while they take in shows and shopping. *145 W. 44th St., 10036, tel. 212/768–4400 or 800/622–5569, fax, 212/767–7693. 638 rooms. Facilities: restaurant, bar/lounge, meeting rooms, corporate dining and meeting suites, fitness center. AE, DC, MC, V.*

The Royalton. Former Studio 54 disco kings Ian Schrager and the late Steve Rubell, in their quest for a second career as New York hotel moguls, completely rehabilitated this once-shabby property directly across from the Algonquin (*see* Moderate, *below*) on West 44th Street off Fifth Avenue. The Royalton, with its witty art moderne design by French decorator Philippe Starck, has a plush but slightly spooky atmosphere: The halls are narrow and dark, as are some of the strangely shaped rooms. Still, the beds and other furnishings are quite comfy, and the bathrooms are decidedly fun—they all have either oversize slate shower stalls or giant circular tubs (a few have both). This could be a delightful spot for a romantic theater weekend for two people with a sense of the absurd. *44 W. 44th St., 10036, tel. 212/869–4400 or 800/635–9013, fax 212/869–8965. 205 rooms. Facilities: restaurant with bar, meeting rooms, game and library areas, VCRs, stereos. AE, DC, MC, V.*

The Waldorf-Astoria. Along with the Plaza (*see* Very Expensive, *above*), this Art Deco masterpiece personifies New York at its most lavish and powerful. Hilton, its owner, has spent a fortune on refurbishing both public areas and guest rooms. Original murals and mosaics, elaborate plaster ornamentation, fine old-wood walls and doors—all look fresh and new. In the guest rooms, some of which start at the low end of this category, there are new bedspreads, carpets, and other signs of upgrading. Bathrooms throughout are old but beautifully kept up and rather spacious by today's standards. Everyone from the Duchess of York to the honeymoon couple from Miami or the salesman from Omaha gets the same amenities; of course, in the very private Tower section, everything becomes just that much grander. There has been a move to modernize the menu at Peacock Alley, where Waldorf salad first made news. Service in the dining areas has improved of late. The hotel's richly tinted, hushed lobby serves as an interior centerpoint of city life; it's nice to see the rest of the place looking proud, too. *301 Park Ave., 10022, tel. 212/355–3000 or 800/HILTONS, fax 212/421–8103. 1,692 rooms. Facilities: 3 restaurants, coffee shop, tearoom, lounge, ballroom, meeting rooms. AE, DC, MC, V.*

Moderate

The Algonquin. While this landmark property's English-drawing-room atmosphere and burnished-wood lobby are being kept intact, its working parts (the plumbing, for instance) are being improved under new Japanese owners. Management is also redecorating, restoring the old mahogany doors and trim, improving the telephone service, and creating a conference and business area. This much-beloved hotel, where the Round Table group of writers and wits once met for lunch, still shelters many a celebrity, particularly literary types visiting nearby publishing houses or the *New Yorker* magazine offices. Late-night performances go on as usual at the Oak Room, with singers such as Julie Wilson and Andrea Marcovicci. Bathrooms and sleeping quarters retain Victorian-style fixtures and furnishings, only now there are larger, firmer beds, modern TVs, VCRs (upon request), computerized phones, and Caswell-Massey toiletries. *59 W. 44th St., 10036, tel. 212/840–6800 or 800/548–0345, fax 212/944–1419. 165 rooms. Facilities: restaurant, 2 lounges, meeting rooms, complimentary parking on weekends, business center. AE, DC, MC, V.*

Journey's End. This Canadian chain's first Manhattan property is what the demanding bargain hunter has been waiting for. No-nonsense, clean, attractive rooms and baths are at one fixed price. Most accommodations come with queen-size beds; all have modern TVs and telephones with long cords. Guests can use a small lounge area for complimentary coffee and newspapers. There is an independently owned Italian restaurant on the premises. At night, this part of midtown is somewhat quiet and therefore prone to street crime. However, security at the hotel appears to be superior. Another plus—it's just a few blocks away from the airport bus departure area on Park Avenue near Grand Central Terminal. *3 E. 40th St., 10016, tel. 212/447–1500 or 800/668–4200. 189 rooms. Facilities: lounge, independent on-premises restaurant, business services on request. AE, DC, MC, V.*

★ **Manhattan Suites East.** Here's a group of good-value properties for the traveler who likes to combine full hotel service with independent pied-à-terre living. These nine midtown hotels have different characters and varying prices, though all fall within the Moderate category. The four best are the recently redone **Beekman Tower** (3 Mitchell Pl.), near the United Nations and on the edge of a trendy East Side residential area; the **Dumont Plaza** (150 E. 34th St.), especially convenient for convention goers with its location on a direct bus line to the Javits Center; the **Surrey Hotel** (20 E. 76th St.), in the neighborhood of Madison Avenue art galleries and designer boutiques; and the **Southgate Tower** (371 7th Ave.), the most attractive and secure place to sleep within close range of Madison Square Garden and Penn Station. Except for the modern style at the Dumont, all have traditional guest-room decor; the Surrey's rooms border on the truly elegant. Most accommodations have pantries, and larger units have dining areas with full-size tables. *Sales office, 505 E. 75th St., 10001, tel. 212/772–2900 or 800/ME-SUITE. AE, DC, MC, V.*

Radisson Empire Hotel. This old hotel recently changed ownership, so it's a matter of time before one knows what's what, but since the new owner is media mogul John Kluge, the Empire should only gain in luster. The English-period lobby is warm and inviting; halls are decorated in soft gray with elegant lamps. Rooms and suites are a bit like small boxes, but nicely furnished; special room features include high-tech electronics, and the small but immaculate baths have heated towel racks. There is a cozy "British" lounge for guests' exclusive use. Although this hotel's prices have gone up, it's still one of the city's better buys in terms of quality and location, right across the street from Lincoln Center. At press time there was no room service, but no matter: The neighborhood is loaded with all-hours dining options. *Broadway at 63rd St., 10023, tel. 212/265-7400, 800/221-6509, or 800/ 223-9868, fax 212/315-0349. 368 rooms. Facilities: restaurant, voice mail. AE, DC, MC, V.*

The Roger Smith Winthrop. The lobby and public areas of this sleeper have been radically remodeled. The guest rooms upstairs are clean, well decorated, and spacious, and special units have small but luxurious marble baths with Jacuzzis. All rooms have pantries, and there's a complimentary Continental breakfast. Guests also receive free passes (one per person) to the Museum of Modern Art. A tea lounge and a new full-service restaurant, Lily's, have recently been added. This is a homey, attractive place to return to at the end of a busy day in midtown. *501 Lexington Ave., 10017, tel. 212/755-1400 or 800/241-3848, fax 212/319-9130. 200 rooms. Facilities: restaurant, meeting room. AE, DC, MC, V.*

The Wyndham. This genteel treasure sits across from The Plaza and adjacent to the Helmsley Park Lane. The savvy, independent traveler who cares more about gracious rooms and a friendly atmosphere than about imposing lobbies and hand-to-mouth service might well choose this spot over its neighbors. Owner and general manager John Mados keeps prices down by not offering room service or fancy amenities; what he does provide are some of the prettiest and most spacious accommodations in Manhattan. Even the least expensive double room has fresh floral-print bedspreads, comfortable chairs, and decorator wall coverings. A slight drawback is the old-fashioned, white-tile bathrooms. *42 W. 58th St., 10019, tel. 212/753-3500, fax 212/754-5638. 201 rooms. Facilities: restaurant. AE, DC, MC, V.*

Inexpensive

Ameritania. This newcomer, a converted single-room-occupancy hotel, is a pleasant choice for the theater goer or business traveler with an eye on the bottom line. At press time, some rooms were still being renovated and services such as the fitness room and restaurant were in the early stages. The lobby is modern and cheerful, as are the simple but well-designed rooms. Some "executive" units have superior baths and amenities. The hotel's proximity to Broadway hits such as *Miss Saigon* and popular night spots such as The Ritz should keep the clientele on the youthful side. *1701 Broadway, 10019, tel. 212/ 247–5000, fax 212/247–3316. 250 rooms. Facilities: restaurant, lounge, fitness room. AE, DC, MC, V.*

Broadway American. The Upper West Side has become one of New York's hottest neighborhoods. Those wishing to be in its midst should try this small but surprisingly stylish lodging. The least expensive singles have shared baths, though most rooms come with private facilities. Decor is functional modern, with high-tech touches such as TVs with cable. The dominating color scheme is soft gray. Baths are basic but no worse than others in more expensive units around town. Everything was clean and new at press time. The only drawback is that some of this former single-room-occupancy hotel's odd-ball occupants are living in old-style rooms not yet converted for transient use. Bearing this possibly unsettling aspect in mind, the Broadway can be recommended for the savings-seeking energetic visitor. *2178 Broadway, 10024, tel. 212/362–1100 or 800/446–4556, fax 212/ 787–9521. 200 rooms. Facilities: independent on-premises restaurant, vending machines, laundry service. AE, DC, MC, V.*

Chatwal Inns. This latest welcome group addition to the Big Apple hotel scene features six properties, located mostly in the Broadway-midtown area, that provide clean, attractively designed rooms at relatively unpainful prices. All guests receive a complimentary Continental breakfast. Some of the larger properties, such as the **Best Western** affiliate (234 W. 48th St.), have on-premises full-service restaurants as

well. Rooms, though relatively small throughout all six hotels, are immaculate and have all
the basic amenities travelers have come to expect, including bathroom toiletries, modern telephones, and TVs. Since many of the buildings
were, until recently, rather dilapidated, don't
be put off by the dingy facades of Chatwal properties like **The Quality Inn Midtown** (157 W.
47th St.) or **The Chatwal Inn** (132 W. 45th St.);
their interiors are among the chain's nicest.
Sant S. Chatwal, owner of Bombay Palace restaurants, is to be applauded for his restoration
and pricing efforts. *Tel. 800/826–4667; in Canada: 800/621–4667. Facilities: restaurants, small
meeting rooms, lounges, depending on the property. AE, DC, MC, V.*

★ **Hotel Edison.** A popular budget stop for tour
groups from here and abroad, this offbeat old
hotel has gotten a face-lift. A gruesome murder
scene for *The Godfather* was shot in what is now
Sophia's restaurant, and the pink plaster coffee
shop has become a hot place to eavesdrop on
show-business gossip thanks to such celebrity
regulars as Jackie Mason. Guest rooms are
brighter and fresher than the dark corridors
seem to hint. There's no room service, but this
part of the theater district has so many restaurants and delis that it doesn't matter much. The
crowd here is perfectly wholesome, so save money on your room and spend the big bucks on better theater seats. *228 W. 47th St., 10036, tel.
212/840–5000. 1,000 rooms. Facilities: restaurant, coffee shop, bar. AE, DC, MC, V.*

★ **Paramount.** What used to be the dowdy Century
Paramount is the latest transformation by the
same team that owns The Royalton (*see* Expensive, *above*). In many ways, this property is both
the better buy and more fun than the more expensive property. The lobby is dramatic; there's
a single wide stairway leading to the mezzanine-
level dining area. The public area seating
groups are at once homey and high style. Even if
you don't dress like David Byrne or Madonna,
you'll feel welcome. Rooms are, as rumored,
rather small, but all of the singles contain
queen-size beds and can certainly be used by
two people. Philippe Starck's furnishings, in
keeping with Ian Schrager's concepts, are offbeat; the old bathrooms have been fixed up with

disco touches like conical steel sinks, and storage areas take a few minutes to decipher. While the Paramount is not for the old-at-heart, it's definitely a category standout. *235 W. 46th St., 10019, tel. 212/764–5500 or 800/225–7474, fax 212/354–5237. 610 rooms. Facilities: two restaurants, privately owned bar, take-out food shop, fitness center, children's playroom, business center, VCRs in rooms. AE, DC, MC, V.*

★ **Vanderbilt YMCA.** Of the various Manhattan Ys offering accommodations, this is the best as far as location and facilities are concerned. Although rooms hold up to four people, they are little more than dormitory-style cells—even with only one or two beds to a room, you may feel crowded. Each room does have a late-model TV, however. There are no private baths; communal showers and toilets are clean. Guests are provided with basics such as towels and soap. Besides the low price, this Y offers instant free membership to its on-premises pool, gym, running track, exercise rooms, and sauna. Many of the athletic and public areas, including the pool, have been remodeled. Rooms are being refreshed, too. An informal cafeteria and a friendly hospitality desk encourage travelers to mix with one another. The Turtle Bay neighborhood is safe, convenient, and interesting (the United Nations is a few short blocks away). Other YMCAs in town include the 561-room **West Side Y** (5 W. 63rd St., 10023, tel. 212/787–4400), which may be hard to get into but is in the desirable Lincoln Center area; and the 1,490-room **Sloane House YMCA** (356 W. 34th St., 10001, tel. 212/760–5860), which is in a gritty and somewhat unsafe neighborhood. *224 E. 47th St., 10017, tel. 212/755–2410. 430 rooms. Facilities: cafeteria, meeting rooms, self-service laundry, gift shop, luggage storage, pool, fitness center. No credit cards.*

Washington Square Hotel. The Village has a surprising paucity of decent budget and midprice lodgings, despite its popularity as a shopping and entertainment district. This cozy hotel has a true European feel and style, from the wrought-iron and brass in the small but elegant lobby, to the personal attention given by the staff. Rooms and baths are simple but pleasant, and feel a bit less "cookie cutter" than those in other hotels in this price range. There is a new bistro on the premises, and within walking distance are abundant coffee shops and convenience stores. The manager has strong ties to the local jazz community and can be especially helpful to those who wish to catch top names at famous clubs such as the nearby Blue Note. Indeed, Bo Diddley and others who could afford fancier digs call this place home when they're making the rounds. *103 Waverly Place, 10011, tel. 212/777–9515 or 800/222–0418, fax 212/979–8373. 160 rooms. Facilities: independent on-premises restaurant, laundry service. AE, DC, MC, V.*

6 The Arts and Nightlife

The Arts

*By Susan
Spano Wells*

*Updated by
Holly Hughes*

Much has been made of the ballooning cost of tickets, especially for Broadway shows—though major concerts and recitals don't come cheap in New York, either. *Miss Saigon* nudged top Broadway ticket prices into the $100 zone, although those seats have since been reduced somewhat with the ailing economy; top tickets for nonmusicals, too, have crept upward, hitting the $50 mark occasionally.

On the positive side, tickets for New York City's arts events aren't hard to come by—unless, of course, you're dead set on seeing the season's hottest, sold-out show. Generally, a theater or concert hall's box office is the best place to buy tickets, since in-house ticket sellers make it their business to know about their theaters and shows and don't mind pointing out (on a chart) where you'll be seated. For advance purchase, send the theater or hall a certified check or money order, several alternate dates, and a self-addressed stamped envelope.

You can also pull out a credit card and call **Tele-Charge** (tel. 212/239–6200), **HIT-TIX** (tel. 212/564–8038), or **Ticketmaster** (tel. 212/307-4100 for Broadway shows, 212/307-7171 for other events) to reserve tickets—newspaper ads generally will specify which you should use for any given event. A small surcharge ($1–$3) will be added to the total, and your tickets will be waiting for you at the theater.

Off- and Off-Off-Broadway theaters have their own joint box office called **Ticket Central** (416 W. 42nd St., tel. 212/279–4200). While there are no discounts here, tickets to performances in these theaters are less expensive than Broadway tickets—Ticket Central prices average $8–$30 per person—and they cover an array of events, including legitimate theater, performance art, and dance.

Discount Tickets The best-known discount source may be the **TKTS booth** in Duffy Square (47th St. and Broadway, tel. 212/354–5800). TKTS sells day-of-performance tickets for Broadway and some Off-Broadway plays at discounts that, depending on a show's popularlty, often go as low as half price (plus a $2 surcharge per ticket). The names of shows available on that day are posted on boards in front of the booth. If you're interested in a Wednesday or Saturday matinee, go to the booth between 10 and 2, check out what's offered, and then wait in line. For evening performances, the booth is open 3–8; for Sunday matinee and evening performances, noon–8. One caution: TKTS accepts only cash or traveler's checks—no credit cards.

A new service has set up operations at **Bloomingdale's** department store (1000 3rd Ave. at 59th St., tel. 212/705–2090), selling tickets to certain Broadway and Off-Broadway shows at discounts of 10% to 75%. The advantages are that it opens at 10 AM, earlier than TKTS, and it accepts credit cards; the disadvantage is that a smaller selection of shows is available. The service charge ranges from $2 to $4.

A setup similar to TKTS has arisen in the **Bryant Park Music and Dance Tickets Booth,** located on 42nd Street in Bryant Park, just west of the New York Public Library. This booth sells half-price day-of-performance tickets for several music and dance events around the city (and full-price tickets for other concerts as well). It's open Tuesday, Thursday, and Friday noon–2 and 3–7; Wednesday and Saturday 11–2 and 3–7; Sunday noon–6. Unlike TKTS, the Bryant Park booth has a telephone information line (tel. 212/382–2323).

Finding Out What's On
To find out who or what's playing where, your first stop should be the newsstand. The *New York Times* isn't a prerequisite for finding out what's going on around town, but it comes in pretty handy, especially on Fridays with its "Weekend" section. On Sundays, the *Times*'s "Arts and Leisure" section features longer "think pieces" on everything from opera to TV—and lots more ads, plus a full, detailed calendar of cultural events for the upcoming week.

If your tastes are more adventurous, try the weekly paper *The Village Voice;* its club listings are unrivaled, its "Choices" section reliable. When its club-tattler-cum-critic Michael Musto talks (in a column called "La Dolce Musto"), night prowlers and club pixies listen. The *Voice* is published on Wednesdays.

Some of the most entertaining listings can be found in *The New Yorker* magazine. "Goings On About Town" heads off each weekly issue with ruthlessly succinct reviews of theater, art, music, film, and nightlife. *New York* magazine's "Cue listings" and "Hot Line" section are useful, too. The *New York Native* and *Outweek* cover the gay scene.

Theater

To most people, New York theater means Broadway, that region bounded by 42nd and 53rd streets, between Sixth and Ninth avenues, where bright, transforming lights shine upon porn theaters and jewel-box playhouses alike. Although the area's busy sidewalks contain more than their share of hustlers and pickpockets, visitors brave them for the playhouses' plentiful delights.

Some of the old playhouses are as interesting for their history as for their current offerings: the **St. James** (246 W. 44th St.) is where Lauren Bacall served as an usherette in the '40s, and a sleeper of a musical called *Oklahoma!* woke up as a hit; the **Lyceum** (149 W. 45th St.) is New York's oldest still-functioning theater, built in 1903 with a posh apartment on top that now holds the Shubert Archive (open to scholars by appointment only); the **Shubert Theatre** (225 W. 44th St.) is where Barbra Streisand made her 1962 Broadway debut, and the long-run record-breaker, *A Chorus Line,* played for 15 years; and the **Martin Beck Theatre** (302 W. 45th St.), built in 1924 in Byzantine style, is the stage that served up premieres of Eugene O'Neill's *The Iceman Cometh,* Arthur Miller's *The Crucible,* and Tennessee Williams's *Sweet Bird of Youth.* Theater names read like a roll-call of American theater history: **Booth, Barrymore, Eugene O'Neill, Gershwin, Lunt/Fontanne, Richard Rodgers,** and **Neil Simon,** among others.

Ten years ago it was relatively simple to categorize the New York stage beyond Broadway. It was divided into Off-Broadway and Off-Off-Broadway, depending on a variety of factors that included theatrical contract type, location, and ticket price. Today such distinctions seem strained, as Off-Broadway prices have risen and the quality of some Off-Off-Broadway productions has improved markedly.

Name actors appear in top-flight productions at **Lincoln Center's** two theaters: the **Vivian Beaumont** and the more intimate **Mitzi E. Newhouse** (65th St. and Broadway, tel. for both 212/362-7600), which has scored some startling successes—witness the long run of John Guare's *Six Degrees of Separation*. Downtown at the **Joseph Papp Public Theater** (425 Lafayette St., tel. 212/598-7150), recently renamed to honor its late founder and long-time guiding genus, artistic director JoAnne Akalaitis continues the tradition of innovative theater, mounting new and classic plays, along with film series, dance concerts, and musical events. In the summertime, the Public's Shakespeare Festival raises its sets in Central Park's open-air Delacorte Theater.

One of the major Off-Broadway enclaves is **Theatre Row,** a collection of small houses (100 seats or less)—such as the **John Houseman Theater** (450 W. 42nd St., tel. 212/967-9077), **Douglas Fairbanks Theater** (432 W. 42nd St., tel. 212/239-4321), and **Playwrights Horizons** (416 W. 42nd St., tel. 212/279-4200)—on the downtown side of 42nd Street between Ninth and Tenth avenues. Another Off-Broadway neighborhood lies in Greenwich Village, around Sheridan Square. Its theaters include **Circle Rep** (99 7th Ave. S, tel. 212/924-7100), a showcase for new playwrights; **Circle in the Square Downtown** (159 Bleecker St., tel. 212/254-6330); the **Lucille Lortel Theater** (121 Christopher St., tel. 212/924-8782); the **Cherry Lane Theater** (38 Commerce St., tel. 212/989-2020); and the **Provincetown Playhouse** (133 MacDougal St., tel. 212/477-5048). Other estimable Off-Broadway theaters are flung across the Manhattan map: the **Promenade Theatre** (Broadway at 76th St., tel. 212/580-1313); the **Roundabout** (100 E. 17th St., tel. 212/420-1883), specializing in revivals of the classics; and the **Manhattan Theatre Club** (at City Center, 131 W. 55th St., tel. 212/581-7907).

Music

Lincoln Center (W. 62nd St. and Broadway) remains the city's musical nerve center, especially when it comes to the classics. The **New York Philharmonic**, led by musical director Kurt Masur, performs at Avery Fisher Hall (tel. 212/875–5030) and will play a number of special gala concerts to celebrate its 150th anniversary season in 1992–93. In summer, the popular **Mostly Mozart** concert series presents an impressive roster of classical performers.

Near Avery Fisher is Alice Tully Hall (tel. 212/875–5050), an intimate "little white box," considered as acoustically perfect as concert houses get. Here the **Chamber Music Society of Lincoln Center** tunes up, along with promising Juilliard students, chamber music ensembles such as the Guarneri Quartet and Kronos Quartet, music on period instruments, choral music, famous soloists, and concert groups.

While Lincoln Center is only 30 years old, another famous classical music palace—**Carnegie Hall** (W. 57th St. at 7th Ave., tel. 212/247–7800)—recently celebrated its 100th birthday. This is the place where the great pianist Paderewski was attacked by ebullient crowds (who claimed kisses and locks of his hair) after a performance in 1891; where young Leonard Bernstein, standing in for New York Philharmonic conductor Bruno Walter, made his triumphant debut in 1943; where Jack Benny and Isaac Stern fiddled together and where the Beatles played one of their first U.S. concerts.

Other prime classical music locales are:

Merkin Concert Hall at the Abraham Goodman House (129 W. 67th St., tel. 212/362–8719), almost as prestigious as the concert halls at Lincoln Center.
Kaufman Concert Hall at the 92nd St. Y (1395 Lexington Ave., tel. 212/415–5440), with the New York Chamber Symphony in residence, plus star recitalists and chamber music groups.
Brooklyn Academy of Music (30 Lafayette Ave., tel. 718/636–4100), ever experimenting with new and old musical styles, and still a showcase for the Brooklyn Philharmonic.

Opera

Recent decades have sharply intensified the public's appreciation for grand opera—partly because of the charismatic personalities of such great singers as Placido Domingo and Beverly Sills, and partly because of the efforts of New York's magnetic **Metropolitan Opera.** A Met premiere draws the rich and famous, the critics, and the connoisseurs. At the Met's elegant Lincoln Center home, with its Marc Chagall murals and weighty Austrian-crystal chandeliers, the supercharged atmosphere gives audiences a sense that something special is going to happen, even before the curtain goes up.

The Metropolitan Opera (tel. 212/362–6000) performs its vaunted repertoire from October to mid-April, and though tickets can cost as much as $125 apiece, standing room is available for far less. Standing room tickets for the week's performance go on sale on Saturday.

Meanwhile, the **New York City Opera,** which performs July–November in Lincoln Center's New York State Theater (tel. 212/870–5570), has faced the departure of its famous general director, Beverly Sills. But with conductor Christopher Keene at the helm, it persists in its "tradition of taking chances on unfamiliar works, old and new" (in the words of *New York Times* critic Donal Henahan) and in nurturing young American stars-to-be. City Opera recently widened its repertoire to include several classic musical comedies, such as *Brigadoon, South Pacific,* and *The Sound of Music,* and it continues its ingenious practice of "supertitling"— electronically displaying, above the stage, line-by-line translations into English for foreign-language operas. Recent seasons have included such time-tested favorites as *Carmen, Madama Butterfly,* and *Rigoletto.*

Dance

The **New York City Ballet,** a hallmark troupe for over 40 years, performs in Lincoln Center's New York State Theater (tel. 212/870–5570). Its season runs from November to February—with December set aside for the beloved annual production of *The Nutcracker*—and from April to June.

Across the plaza at Lincoln Center, the Metropolitan Opera House (tel. 212/362–6000) is home to the **American Ballet Theatre,** noted especially for its brilliant renditions of story ballets and its lyrical style, as well as its world-renowned featured dancers. Its season opens in April, when the opera season closes, and runs through June.

When the ABT and NYCB take a break from performing, Lincoln Center acts as impresario for dozens of world-renowned companies, such as the Bolshoi and Royal Danish ballets.

The varied bill at **City Center** (131 W. 55th St., tel. 212/581–7907) often includes touring ballet companies; recently the Matsuyama Ballet from Japan performed there.

A growing modern dance center is the **Joyce Theater** (175 8th Ave., tel. 212/242–0800), housed in a former Art Deco movie theater. The Joyce is the permanent home of **Feld Ballets/NY,** founded in 1974 by an upstart ABT dancer who went on to become a principal fixture on the dance scene. Other featured companies include the **Nikolais and Murray Louis Dance Company,** the avant-garde **ZeroMoving Company,** and the loony acrobats of **Pilobolus.** At **Symphony Space** (2537 Broadway, tel. 212/864–1414), the bill features ethnic dance.

Here's a sampling of other, mostly experimental and avant-garde, dance forums:

Dance Theater Workshop (219 W. 19th St., tel. 212/691–6500), one of New York's most successful laboratories for new dance.
Danspace Project (at St. Mark's-in-the-Bowery Church, 10th St. and 2nd Ave., tel. 212/529–2318), with a series of avant-garde and historical choreography that runs from September to June.
DIA Center for the Arts (155 Mercer St., tel. 212/431–9232) hosts a number of performances by interesting local dancers.
P.S. 122 (150 1st Ave., tel. 212/477–5288), where dance events border on performance art; among others, Meredith Monk occasionally cavorts here.

Film

The Times Square area is still a movie mecca, though action flicks prevail on 42nd Street, and viewers should be warned to sit tight and hold on to their purses. Posh East Side first-run theaters line Third Avenue between 57th and 60th streets and continue up Second Avenue into the 60s. Other groups are clustered around East 34th Street, West 23rd Street, and Broadway between 60th and 63rd streets.

Revival Houses The biggest news for old-movie buffs in New York City is the 1991 opening of the **Walter Reade Theater** in Lincoln Center (70 Lincoln Center Plaza, tel. 212/875–5600), operated by the Film Society of Lincoln Center. Several fascinating series run concurrently, along such themes as Depression-era movies, famous directors' first movies, and Saturday morning movies for kids; the auditorium is a little gem, and tickets can be purchased at the box office weeks in advance.

Revivals can also be found at:

Cinema Village Third Avenue (100 3rd Ave., between 12th and 13th Sts., tel. 212/505–7320) and its sister theater **Cinema Village 12th Street** (12th St. between 5th Ave. and University Pl., tel. 212/924–3364), offering reshowings of lesser-known films that are a few years old.
Eighth Street Playhouse (52 W. 8th St., tel. 212/674–6515), screening revivals along with new foreign and independent movies.
Film Forum (209 W. Houston St., tel. 212/727–8110), with three screens showing often quirky series based on movie genres, directors, and other film artists.
Theatre 80 St. Marks (80 St. Marks Pl., tel. 212/254–7400), small and shabby but convivial, specializing in double-features from the '30s and '40s.
The Museum of Modern Art (11 W. 53rd St., tel. 212/708–9480), which includes classic films in its many series.

Foreign and Independent Films **Angelika Film Center** (Houston and Mercer Sts., tel. 212/995–2000), which devotes at least a couple of its screens to the kind of fare that attracts film students from nearby New York University.

Carnegie Hall Cinema and **Carnegie Hall Screening Room** (887 7th Ave. between 56th and 57th Sts., tel. 212/265–2520), where intriguing new films find long runs.

Eighth Street Playhouse (52 W. 8th St., tel. 212/674–6515), screening revivals along with new foreign and independent movies.

Lincoln Plaza (Broadway between 62nd and 63rd Sts., tel. 212/757–2280), three subterranean cinemas playing long-run foreign hits.

The Plaza (42 E. 58th St., tel. 212/355–3320), a showcase for much-talked-about new American and foreign entries.

The Public Theater (425 Lafayette St., tel. 212/598–7171), a reliable forum for experimental and independent film.

68th Street Playhouse (3rd Ave. at 68th St., tel. 212/734–0302), with exclusive extended runs of critically acclaimed films.

Quad Cinema (13th St. between 5th and 6th Aves., tel. 212/255–8800), with first-run Hollywood, art, and foreign films.

Nightlife

Clubs and Entertainment

By Susan Spano Wells

Updated by Terry Trucco

On Friday, the *New York Times*'s "Weekend" section carries a "Sounds Around Town" column that can give you a picture of what's in the air, as can the *Village Voice*, which probably has more nightclub ads than any rag in the world. Or stop by Tower Records (692 Broadway, tel. 212/505–1500, and 1961 Broadway, tel. 212/799–2500), where fliers about coming events and club passes are stacked outside. You may also get good tips from a suitably au courant hotel concierge. Just remember that what's hot and what's not changes almost weekly in this city, so visitors are at a distinct disadvantage. We've tried to give you a rounded sample of reliable hangouts—establishments that are likely to be still in business by the time you use this book—but clubs come and go as fast as spawning tsetse flies, so phone ahead to make sure your target night spot hasn't closed or turned into a polka hall. Most will charge a cover of at least $10 a head; some go as high as $20–$50 (nobody said catting around was going to be cheap!). Take cash because many places don't accept plastic. *Et maintenant, mesdames et messieurs*, what's your choice?

Putting on the Ritz   **The Ballroom** (253 W. 28th St., tel. 212/244–3005). This very hip Chelsea spot has an extensive tapas bar and a nightclub where some of the great chanteuses—including Peggy Lee and Helen Schneider—rhapsodize.

The Carlyle (35 E. 76th St., tel. 212/744–1600). The hotel's discreetly sophisticated Café Carlyle is where Bobby Short plays when he's in town; Bemelmans' Bar, with murals by the author of the Madeleine books, regularly stars jazz pianist Barbara Carroll.

Nell's (246 W. 14th St., tel. 212/675–1567). Back in vogue, Nell Campbell (of *Rocky Horror* fame) reintroduced sophistication to nightlife with her club. The tone in the upstairs jazz salon is Victorian; downstairs is for tête-à-têtes and dancing.

The Oak Room (at the Algonquin Hotel, 59 W. 44th St., tel. 212/840–6800). Please don't gawk at the famous writers as you come in. Just head straight for the long, narrow club-cum-watering hole; at the piano you'll find, perhaps, singer Julie Wilson, the hopelessly romantic Andrea Marcovicci, or showtune chanteuse Iris Williams.

The Rainbow Room and **Rainbow and Stars Club** (30 Rockefeller Plaza, tel. 212/632–5000). You can find two kinds of heaven high up on Rockefeller Center's 65th floor. The Rainbow Room serves dinner and dancing to the strains of a live orchestra takes place on a floor right out of an Astaire/Rogers musical. At the intimate new Rainbow and Stars Club, singers such as Tony Bennett and Liliane Montevecchi entertain, backlit by a view of the twinkling lights of the city.

Jazz Notes   **The Blue Note** (131 W. 3rd St., tel. 212/475–8592). This club may be the jazz capital of the world. Just an average week could bring Irma Thomas, the Modern Jazz Quartet, and Dizzy Gillespie. If jazz is your thing, make a beeline to the Blue Note.

Bradley's (70 University Pl., tel. 212/228–6440). With brighter-than-usual lighting and, generally, jazz piano, this is a spot for serious fans of jazz and blues.

The Kitchen (512 W. 19th St., tel. 212/255–5793). The home of the downtown arts features jazz mixed with a little New Music and World Beat.

The Knitting Factory (47 E. Houston St., tel. 212/219–3055). It looks seedy on the outside, but inside there's often fine avant-gardish jazz.

The Village Gate (Bleecker and Thompson Sts., tel. 212/475–5120). This is another of the classic Village jazz joints. Music starts at 9:30 PM. Upstairs there's a cabaret theater.

The Village Vanguard (178 7th Ave. S, tel. 212/255–4037). This old Thelonius Monk haunt lives on in a smoky cellar until recently presided over by the late jazz impresario Max Gordon. It's pricey, but worth every penny.

Rock Around the Clock

CBGB & OMFUG (315 Bowery, tel. 212/982–4052). American punk rock was born here, in this long black tunnel of a club featuring bands with inventive names: Blind Idiot God, Rude Buddhas, Chemical Wedding. Repair your ears and your appetites at the Pizza Boutique next door.

Palladium (126 E. 14th St., tel. 212/473–7171). Here you'll find the world's biggest dance floor, fashioned from the gutted hulk of a theater, along a New Wave/Oriental '60s-psychedelic theme. Home to the V.I.P. Mike Todd room, Lambada fever, and Club MTV, it is no longer the hot ticket it was a few years ago; still, this place is to clubland what Macy's is to shopping.

The Ritz (254 W. 54th St., tel. 212/541–8900). There must be something magical about the former site of Studio 54; this club is just as popular but not quite as infamous as its predecessor. Weeknight shows begin at 9 PM; the main floor is for dancing, with seating in the balcony. The Ritz turns into a nightclub called Clubland after concerts or on nonconcert evenings.

Wetlands Preserve (161 Hudson St., tel. 212/966–4225). Billed as a "watering hole for activists," this relative newcomer specializes in psychedelic rock. There are Grateful Dead nights on Tuesdays, and "Eco-Saloons" on Sundays.

Comic Relief **Catch a Rising Star** (1487 1st Ave., tel. 212/794–1906). Johnny Carson got his start here, and his talent scouts still show up to test the comic current. This place is neither trendy nor cutting edge, but it is reliable.

Chicago City Limits (351 E. 74th St., tel. 212/772–8707). This troupe's been doing improvisational comedy for a long time, and it seldom fails to whip its mostly youngish audiences into a laughing frenzy. Chicago City Limits performs in an East Side church and is very strong on audience participation.

The Improvisation (358 W. 44th St., tel. 212/765–8268). The Improv is to comedy what the Blue Note is to jazz. Lots of now-famous comedians got their first laughs here, among them Richard Pryor and Robin Williams. It gets crowded, especially on weekends; there are two shows on Fridays and three on Saturday nights.

Bars

Vintage Classics **The Algonquin Hotel Lounge** (59 W. 44th St., tel. 212/840–6800). This is a venerable spot, not only because it was the site of the fabled literary Round Table, but also for its elegant tone. A fabulous grandfather clock tolls the passing hours, while noted writers still come and go.

Elaine's (1703 2nd Ave., tel. 212/534–8103). The food's nothing special, and you will be relegated to an inferior table, but go to crane your neck and gawk. Woody Allen's favorite table is by the cappuccino machine. It's best to visit late, when the stars rise in Elaine's firmament.

King Cole Bar (at the St. Regis Hotel, 2 E. 55th St., tel. 212/753–4500.) The famed Maxwell Parrish mural is a welcome sight at this midtown landmark, happily open again following a thorough and sensitive restoration.

Windows on the World (1 World Trade Center, tel. 212/938–1111). To borrow Cole Porter's words: "You're a Botticelli, you're Keats, you're Shelley . . . you're the top." Here, you'll be 107 stories up, drinking in your favorite poison and the outstanding view.

Drinking Spots Around Town

Chelsea and the Village

Cedar Tavern (82 University Pl., tel. 212/243–9355). Here's a very informal, warm spot for a post-double-feature beer. Years ago, this was the hangout of choice for a generation of New York painters.

Chumley's (86 Bedford St., tel. 212/675–4449). There's no sign to help you find this place—they took it down during Chumley's speakeasy days. A fireplace warms this relaxed spot where the burgers are hearty, and the kitchen stays open past 10 PM.

Coffee Shop (29 Union Square W., tel. 212/243–7969). A hip, 23-hour-a-day hangout, the place lures funky types, beautiful-people-in-training, and a few aging locals who frequented the place when it was a real coffeeshop.

McSorley's Old Ale House (15 E. 7th St., tel. 212/473–9148). One of New York's oldest saloons (opened in 1854), this place has its own satisfying label of ale. Weekend nights are boisterous; on Sunday afternoons McSorley's offers quaint surroundings for reading the paper and munching on a plate of the house specialty, onions and cheese.

The White Horse Tavern (567 Hudson St., tel. 212/243–9260). Famous among the literati, this is the place where Dylan Thomas drained his last cup to the dregs. From April to October, there's outdoor café drinking.

Midtown and the Theater District

Barrymore's (267 W. 45th St., tel. 212/391–8400). This is a pleasantly downscale theater-district spot, with the requisite show posters on the wall. Listen in to the conversations at the bar and you'll hear the tawdry, true stories of what goes on behind gilt prosceniums.

Hard Rock Café (221 W. 57th St., tel. 212/459–9230). Embraced by the kids of stars—in fact, its clientele seems eternally prepubescent—this place is big, popular, and far too noisy for talk.

Joe Allen (326 W. 46th St., tel. 212/581–6464). At this old reliable on Restaurant Row, everybody's en route to or from a show.

The Landmark Tavern (626 11th Ave., tel. 212/757–8595). This aged pub (opened in 1868) is blessed by the glow of warming fireplaces.

P.J. Clarke's (915 3rd Ave., tel. 212/759–1650). New York's most famous Irish bar, this bar comes complete with the requisite mirrors and polished wood. Lots of after-workers like unwinding here, in a place that recalls the days of Tammany Hall.

Planet Hollywood (140 W. 57th St., tel. 212/333–7827). It's touristy, and waiting lines are long. Still, the place has cachet and an undeniable star quality, despite the very compact bar.

Sardi's (234 W. 44th St., tel. 212/221–8440). If you care for the theater, don't leave New York without visiting this establishment, which is as much a fixture in the theater district as the playhouses themselves. Looking like some grande dame of the theater, this recently renovated landmark has beefed up its wine list and added "light" cuisine to its menu, but continues to serve venerable dishes that are all but extinct, amidst its caricature-covered walls.

The Whiskey (at the Paramount Hotel, 235 W. 46th St., tel. 212/764–5500). Finally, a liquor license—and bar—for this chic, revamped Times Square hotel. The downstairs Whiskey, sleek and hip, is ideal après-theater. Also fun for evening drinks is the mezzanine lounge, pure Philippe Starck-meets-the-'40s. Wear black.

East Side **Jim McMullen's** (1341 3rd Ave., tel. 212/861–4700). A young, quintessential Upper East Side watering hole, McMullen's has a large, busy bar decked with bouquets of fresh flowers. Here you'll find lots of Gold Cards, tennis talk, and alumni fund gathering.

Mark's Bar (at Mark Hotel, 25 E. 77th St., tel. 212/879–1864). This sleek East Side bar in a sleek East Side hotel attracts monied Europeans and—what else?—sleek East Siders.

The Polo Lounge (at the Westbury Hotel, 15 E. 69th St., tel. 212/535–9141). This place is, in a word, classy; it's frequented by European royalty and Knickerbocker New York.

West Side **The Conservatory** (at the Mayflower Hotel, 15 Central Park West, tel. 212/581–1293). Furnished, perhaps, out of a Bloomingdale's window, this is reputedly the haunt of Hollywood movie barons in town to cut deals. Beyond all that, it's a pleasant, quiet place in which to talk and drink.

Dublin House (225 W. 79th St., tel. 212/874–9528). Above the door glows a small neon harp;

inside you'll find lots of very young professionals, Columbia students, and softball teams throwing back two-bit drafts.

Lucy's Restaurant (503 Columbus Ave., tel. 212/787–3009). This Southern California-Mex hangout is a hit with young Upper West Siders, who pack themselves into the bar area and sometimes even manage to dance. The decor is playful Gulf beach hut.

Gay Bars
Crazy Nanny (21 7th Ave. S., tel. 212/366–6312). Even in wide-open New York, women's bars aren't easy to find. This one's small, but that doesn't discourage the die-hard jukebox dancers.

The Eagle (142 11th Ave., tel. 212/691–8451). The hormones are always running at this favorite cruise bar, attracting a balanced mix of types, including pool players and dancing fools (there's a DJ on board).

Julius (159 W. 10th St., tel. 212/929–9672). Warm, friendly, and low-key, Julius was one of the first bars on the gay scene; it's renowned for its beefy "Julius Burger." The crowd's a little older now, but the place still offers respite from more frenetic atmospheres.

Marie's Crisis (59 Grove St., tel. 212/243–9323). You've got to love it for its name, and for its ecstatic piano sing-alongs—everybody seems to know all the words to Stephen Sondheim's musical *Sunday in the Park with George*.

Uncle Charlie's Downtown (56 Greenwich Ave., tel. 212/255–8787). This extremely popular Village gay bar is visited by stylish young men and distinguished-looking professionals. Happy hour on weeknights between 5 and 8 packs them in.

Index

Personal Itinerary

Departure *Date*

Time

Transportation

Arrival *Date*   *Time*

Departure *Date*   *Time*

Transportation

Accommodations

Arrival *Date*   *Time*

Departure *Date*   *Time*

Transportation

Accommodations

Arrival *Date*   *Time*

Departure *Date*   *Time*

Transportation

Accommodations

Personal Itinerary

Arrival *Date*   *Time*

Departure *Date*   *Time*

Transportation

Accommodations

Arrival *Date*   *Time*

Departure *Date*   *Time*

Transportation

Accommodations

Arrival *Date*   *Time*

Departure *Date*   *Time*

Transportation

Accommodations

Arrival *Date*   *Time*

Departure *Date*   *Time*

Transportation

Accommodations

Personal Itinerary

Arrival *Date*   *Time*

Departure *Date*   *Time*

Transportation

Accommodations

Arrival *Date*   *Time*

Departure *Date*   *Time*

Transportation

Accommodations

Arrival *Date*   *Time*

Departure *Date*   *Time*

Transportation

Accommodations

Arrival *Date*   *Time*

Departure *Date*   *Time*

Transportation

Accommodations

Addresses

Name

Address

Telephone

Name

Address

Telephone

Name

Address

Telephone

Name

Address

Telephone

Name

Address

Telephone

Name

Address

Telephone

Name

Address

Telephone

Name

Address

Telephone

Name

Address

Telephone

Name

Address

Telephone

Name

Address

Telephone

Name

Address

Telephone

Name

Address

Telephone

Name

Address

Telephone

Name

Address

Telephone

Name

Address

Telephone

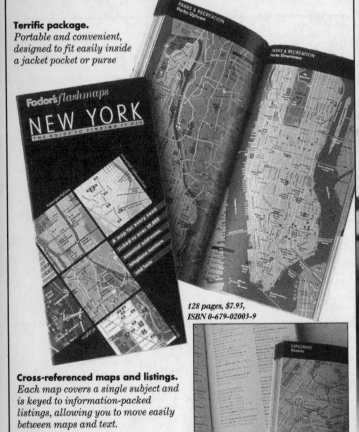

Fodor's Travel Guides

U.S. Guides

Alaska

Arizona

Boston

California

Cape Cod, Martha's
Vineyard, Nantucket

The Carolinas & the
Georgia Coast

Chicago

Disney World & the
Orlando Area

Florida

Hawaii

Las Vegas, Reno,
Tahoe

Los Angeles

Maine, Vermont,
New Hampshire

Maui

Miami & the Keys

New England

New Orleans

New York City

Pacific North Coast

Philadelphia & the
Pennsylvania Dutch
Country

San Diego

San Francisco

Santa Fe, Taos,
Albuquerque

Seattle & Vancouver

The South

The U.S. & British
Virgin Islands

The Upper Great
Lakes Region

USA

Vacations in New York
State

Vacations on the
Jersey Shore

Virginia & Maryland

Waikiki

Washington, D.C.

Foreign Guides

Acapulco, Ixtapa,
Zihuatanejo

Australia & New
Zealand

Austria

The Bahamas

Baja & Mexico's
Pacific Coast Resorts

Barbados

Berlin

Bermuda

Brazil

Budapest

Budget Europe

Canada

Cancun, Cozumel,
Yucatan Penisula

Caribbean

Central America

China

Costa Rica, Belize,
Guatemala

Czechoslovakia

Eastern Europe

Egypt

Euro Disney

Europe

Europe's Great Cities

France

Germany

Great Britain

Greece

The Himalayan
Countries

Hong Kong

India

Ireland

Israel

Italy

Italy's Great Cities

Japan

Kenya & Tanzania

Korea

London

Madrid & Barcelona

Mexico

Montreal &
Quebec City

Morocco

The Netherlands
Belgium &
Luxembourg

New Zealand

Norway

Nova Scotia, Prince
Edward Island &
New Brunswick

Paris

Portugal

Rome

Russia & the Baltic
Countries

Scandinavia

Scotland

Singapore

South America

Southeast Asia

South Pacific

Spain

Sweden

Switzerland

Thailand

Tokyo

Toronto

Turkey

Vienna & the Danube
Valley

Yugoslavia